T0334351

Cambridge Elements ≡

Elements in Crime Narratives
edited by
Margot Douaihy
Emerson College
Catherine Nickerson
Emory College of Arts and Sciences
Henry Sutton
University of East Anglia

BLOODLINES

Adoption, Crime, and the Search for Belonging

Jinny Huh
University of Vermont

CAMBRIDGE
UNIVERSITY PRESS

CAMBRIDGE
UNIVERSITY PRESS

Shaftesbury Road, Cambridge CB2 8EA, United Kingdom

One Liberty Plaza, 20th Floor, New York, NY 10006, USA

477 Williamstown Road, Port Melbourne, VIC 3207, Australia

314–321, 3rd Floor, Plot 3, Splendor Forum, Jasola District Centre,
New Delhi – 110025, India

103 Penang Road, #05–06/07, Visioncrest Commercial, Singapore 238467

Cambridge University Press is part of Cambridge University Press & Assessment,
a department of the University of Cambridge.

We share the University's mission to contribute to society through the pursuit
of education, learning and research at the highest international levels of excellence.

www.cambridge.org
Information on this title: www.cambridge.org/9781009547864

DOI: 10.1017/9781009360999

First published 2025

A catalogue record for this publication is available from the British Library

ISBN 978-1-009-54786-4 Hardback
ISBN 978-1-009-36096-8 Paperback
ISSN 2755-1873 (online)
ISSN 2755-1865 (print)

Bloodlines

Adoption, Crime, and the Search for Belonging

Elements in Crime Narratives

DOI: 10.1017/9781009360999
First published online: January 2025

Jinny Huh
University of Vermont

Author for correspondence: Jinny Huh, Jinny.Huh@uvm.edu

Abstract: This study explores the relationship between crime fiction and adoption. A primary goal of this study is to investigate how the adoption trope reveals current cultural fears and fascination with kinship formations and essentialist notions of belonging, DNA and ancestry searches, and the controversial practice of adoption. Popular fiction, namely crime/detective fiction and the subgenre of adoption crime fiction, reflect scholarly debates within the field of Critical Adoption Studies, including but not limited to the ethics behind the adoption industrial complex and calls for its demise, struggles for reproductive justice, and redefinitions of parenting and kinship formations evidenced by LGBTQ and racialized identities. Another goal of this study is to highlight adoptee and birthparent voices and perspectives, illustrating how genre fiction can help to agitate for more inclusive representation. By intersecting elements of crime into the adoption story, these narratives illuminate the human cost and condition of current adoption practices.

Keywords: adoption and crime, transracial adoption, DNA and ancestry, mothering and race, family secrets

ISBNs: 9781009547864 (HB), 9781009360968 (PB), 9781009360999 (OC)
ISSNs: 2755-1873 (online), 2755-1865 (print)

Contents

Introduction

Broken Harts

The first time I saw Devonte Hart was in the viral 2014 image of him holding tightly to a police officer. Twelve-year-old Devonte was at a protest in Portland, Oregon, shortly after a grand jury decided against indicting the police officer who shot and killed Michael Brown. With tears running down his face and a look of deep pain in his eyes, Devonte was holding a Free Hugs sign when Sgt. Bret Barnum approached him. After a brief conversation, Barnum asked for a hug, which Devonte readily and tearfully gave. This image of a young Black boy and a White police officer became a symbol of racial unity amid heightened racial tensions. One Facebook writer wrote of the image, "I really believe in my heart that this is what most people want – to find the common good in all people and find things we can agree on, not fight about . . . I love this picture and wish that little boy the best life has to offer" (Grinberg). Tragically, four years after this picture was taken, Devonte, along with his five siblings, was murdered at the hands of their adoptive mother.

One of the most heart-wrenching stories in recent years is the Hart family murders. In March 2018, Jennifer Hart drove her car off a Mendocino, California, cliff, killing herself, her wife, Sarah Hart, and their six adopted children. In 2019, a coroner's inquest determined that Jennifer and Sarah Hart committed murder-suicide. According to coroner reports, Jennifer was legally drunk with a blood alcohol level of 0.10 percent when she was behind the wheel. Sarah and three children found in the car wreckage – Markis, 19, Jeremiah, 14, Abigail, 14 – had toxic levels of diphenhydramine, an active ingredient in the antihistamine Benadryl, in their systems. The remains of Ciera, 12, and Hannah, 16, were discovered weeks after the accident. Devonte, 15, has yet to be found but is presumed to be dead.

As more information is revealed about the intricacies of this tragic case, it is clear that a series of misconduct, abuse, and neglect by the adoptive parents were ignored or found legally inconclusive for years prior to their deaths. Behind images of the perfect, peace-loving family regularly displayed on social media, Jennifer and Sarah Hart routinely evaded allegations of child abuse and criminal investigations by moving across several states. Records show that prior to the tragic deaths, the Harts were fleeing child protective services when they drove off the California cliff.

Perhaps more tragically, the events that led to the adoption of these six children reveal what the acclaimed legal scholar Dorothy Roberts calls the racialized disparities of family policing in the child welfare system (see Roberts). As White adoptive lesbian parents with transracially adopted children, the Hart family tragedy reveals intersections of White liberalism, a system of racial injustice that disenfranchised the children's birth families, and criticisms against a foster care system and adoption industry that routinely fail our children. In her widely researched investigation of the Hart family, journalist Roxanna Asgarian reveals a system that, unfortunately, did not protect these six victims. In *We Were Once a Family: A Story of Love, Death, and Child Removal in America* (2023), Asgarian reveals the birth family stories of both sets of siblings to expose a system that routinely damages Black and Brown families by favoring separation and incarceration over reunification and rehabilitation. Asgarian's meticulous enquiry details how although the child welfare system's priority is to safeguard children, the Hart family case illustrates the exact opposite.

> But the Hart family story complicates popular narratives about abuse and the role of CPS in protecting children from it. The children's birth families were not beating their children or starving them; they were clearly struggling with substance use and mental illness, but instead of receiving help, the parents were punished. On the other hand, authorities consistently projected a halo of goodness onto the adoptive mothers, throughout a decade of abuse allegations and even after the murder of their children, with cops and other officials bending over backward to interpret their actions in the kindest possible light. (268)

To be clear, many were fooled into believing that Jennifer and Sarah Hart, White progressive lesbians, provided their six adopted Black children with the insight and strength necessary to be Black in America. Representing themselves as social justice advocates, the family regularly attended protests against police brutality, political rallies for Bernie Sanders, and music festivals centering peace and harmony. We will never know why Jennifer and Sarah Hart chose to adopt. Was it financial incentives or, perhaps, performing a certain type of liberal progressive image? Whatever the reasons, we were too late in helping the Hart children.

As a transracial adoptive mother who had recently undergone the adoption process, I remember being simultaneously shocked and angry when I heard about the Hart tragedy. How and why could this happen? How did we *allow* this to happen? Why didn't anyone listen to the children? As someone who had very little awareness of adoption prior to our own adoption in 2010, I turned to my academic expertise in research to intellectually engage with my anger and sense of helplessness. As a literature professor, I am a lover of words and stories; I sought out novels, memoirs, and critical studies (history, sociology, law) to educate myself on the history and cultural phenomenon of adoption in the U.S. What I found was a surprising mountain of evidence that not only revealed the range of various crimes in the adoption industrial complex but also appeals from the adoption triad, especially adoptees, to be heard and understood. Examined together, the line between obvious crime (child trafficking) and not-so-obvious crime (the legal mandate of sealing adoption records) became blurred. *Bloodlines: Adoption, Crime, and the Search for Belonging* is the result of this investigation, an intersection of the personal with the professional, written with a transracial adoptive mother/Black, Indigenous, and Women of Color (BIWOC) and social justice-centered/academic gaze at its critical core.[1]

Adoption and Crime

Adoption is multi-faceted and different for every family. There is no single adoption story. People who enter into the adoption world for the first time as potential parents or as loved ones of an adoption triad member may be surprised to discover the myriad of not-so-flattering stories of adoption in the headlines and popular media. Intermixed with the story of a couple who desires to become parents via adoption are images of adoption intricately connected to some type of criminal undercurrent, mostly child trafficking and corrupt adoption agencies or negligent birthmothers incapable of mothering. Recent studies on early twentieth-century adoption practices leading into contemporary realities have forced us to accept and be accountable to how children have been separated from their birth families. One major reality is child trafficking. Several recent headlines evidence how common child trafficking has become in countries that profit from international adoption. Stories of sisters kidnapped from temporary orphanages in India (Goldman) and a Chilean birthmother who was told her son died at the hospital only to learn years later that he was stolen in a government/church/hospital-sanctioned plot to traffic children ("Adopted") illustrate the thriving presence and business of child trafficking. In the U.S., perhaps no other individual has impacted the modern adoption industry than Georgia Tann. Trained in law and social work, Tann operated the Tennessee Children's Home Society from 1924 to 1950. She was nationally recognized as *the* expert in adoption, speaking at national conferences, advising First Lady Eleanor Roosevelt, mingling with President Harry Truman, and facilitating adoptions for celebrity clients like Joan Crawford, Mary Pickford, Dick Powell, and June Allyson. But, it was revealed that through her eugenics-based prejudices, exploitation of the poor, and lack of adoption regulation, Tann profited from

---

[1] A heartfelt thanks to the anonymous reader who pointed out that my surprise and unawareness highlighted in this paragraph is a privilege and oftentimes offensive to adoptees. My intent is not to offend but rather to reveal and acknowledge the very ignorance the reader identifies. In some ways, this study is a reflection of my self-education and will hopefully help others, both members of the adoption triad and outsiders, recognize their own assumptions and privileges as well.

trafficking, abusing (sometimes killing), and commercializing children.[2] By the time Tann's corruption was uncovered, it was estimated that approximately 5,000 children were affected. Because Tann's co-conspirators were powerful figures in Tennessee (politicians, doctors, social workers, judges), investigations into her agency were stalled with the Public Acts of 1951, which made all adoption records confidential until 1995 (Hsiao).[3]

A resounding gap in adoption studies is the inclusion of birthmother perspectives and experiences. Ann Fessler's *The Girls Who Went Away* (2006) is a moving account of thousands of American women between World War II and *Roe v. Wade* who were socially/religiously/politically pressured to relinquish their babies. Studies like Fessler's reveal that birthmothers experience a prolonged and unforgettable sense of loss and trauma, underscoring their humanity in an oftentimes heartless industry. Both Fessler's award-winning investigation and the revelation of Tann's corruption expose how the emergence of adoption as an institutional practice is inextricably linked to criminal and corrupt foundations frequently supported and sustained by legal, government, healthcare, and religious institutions.

In addition to domestic corruption, recent studies of international adoption practices unveil the widespread exploitation and fraud in the industry. Erin Siegal is an investigative journalist who uncovers Guatemala's black market adoption industry via two mothers' perspectives, an American adoptive mother and a poor Guatemalan mother whose daughters were stolen from her. In *Finding Fernanda: Two Mothers, One Child, and A Cross-Border Search for Truth*, Siegal uncovers Guatemala's multi-million-dollar adoption industry that, lacking in regulation and full of corrupt conspirators, works in conjunction with American Christian adoption agencies to traffic children. In *China's Hidden Children: Abandonment, Adoption, and the Human Costs of the One-Child Policy* (2016), Kay Ann Johnson investigates China's one child policy as a "population project" (6) and its effects on the circulation of children via forced abandonment or "coerced choice" (19), local and informal adoptions (by other relatives, neighbors, friends), and concealment of unregistered births known as "black children." With the implementation of the state adoption law in 1992 that forbid local adoptions coupled with threats of punishment for having more than one child (including forced sterilization), birthmothers relinquished

---

[2] See Lisa Wingate's award-winning *Before We Were Yours* (2017) for a fictionalization of Tann and the Tennessee Children's Home Society.

[3] See also Barbara Bisantz Raymond's *The Baby Thief: The Untold Story of Georgia Tann, the Baby Seller Who Corrupted Adoption* and Gabrielle Glaser's *American Baby: A Mother, A Child, and the Secret History of Adoption*.

approximately 120,000 babies, many of whom were trafficked out to international adoptions (80,000 to the U.S.).

Of course, racial controversies behind adoption are inescapable in the U.S. The Hart family tragedy above became international news in 2018, bringing new attention to transracial adoption and, in particular, how the Hart children's earlier allegations of abuse were ignored. We cannot truly comprehend how the Hart children were ultimately passed through and neglected by a fundamentally racist child welfare system without studies like Dorothy Roberts's *Torn Apart: How the Child Welfare System Destroys Black Families* (2022) or her earlier study, *Shattered Bonds: The Color of Child Welfare* (2001). Roberts, esteemed professor of law, sociology, and civil rights at the University of Pennsylvania, calls for abolishing the child welfare system that relies on racist myths and slavery-originated policies to punish and police Black families. For the adoption industry to recognize that many of the Black and Brown available children are the subsequent consequences of a racist system that *benefits from* the destruction of the Black family would be, to say the least, transformative. This acknowledgment would also offer additional perspective to the 1972 National Association of Black Social Workers Position Statement, which called the practice of Black children adopted by White parents as "genocide" (National).[4]

From the ugly history of the past coupled with the ongoing trauma of a welfare system that breaks apart families as well as economic networks that both legally and illegally recognize, practice, and sanction the separation of children from their birthfamilies, I cannot help but be reminded of the thousands of children who are culturally and legally coerced into being silently satisfied with their adoptee positionality. Many cannot still access legal documents such as their original birth certificates. Some, like the Hart children, are silenced forever. It is not surprising then that movements like #abolishadoption, led by adoptees, advocate for establishing kinship legal guardianship as an alternative to adoption. #flipthescript (which I elaborate on in Section Two) is another movement that calls to center adoptee voices and perspectives. As a transracial adoptive motherscholar, *Bloodlines* is my small attempt to acknowledge and share widely how adoption as a cultural phenomenon has been a source of anxiety and fear. As a transracial adoptive mother whose daughter is currently navigating her own questions and confusions about her adoptee identity, *Bloodlines* is also my way of telling her, *I see you, I hear you, I love you.*

---

[4] See Laura Briggs's *Somebody's Children: The Politics of Transracial and Transnational Adoption* (2012) for additional background on the social and cultural forces, including poverty, racism, and political violence, that shaped and made possible transracial and transnational adoption in the U.S.

Section Outline

It is no wonder that alongside this troubling history, popular responses and representations such as literary studies reflect anxieties of crime and corruption in adoption practices. Section 1 details some common adoption stigmas and its fictional representations in contemporary crime fiction. Closely examining themes such as child trafficking, "real" versus adopted families, anxieties about birthmothers, nontraditional family formations such as surrogacy, and the disturbing practice of rehoming, this section highlights some of the biggest fears and failures resulting in popular speculations around adoption. Who are the "real" parents? What happens if the birthmother is "unbalanced" and/or changes her mind? What if the adoptee cannot assimilate into the adopted home? Questions like these not only expose our cultural assumptions behind adoption and kinship formation but also help to maintain the insensitive lack of awareness behind adoption trauma and loss.[5]

While Section 1 foregrounds the fears and nightmares of adoption in crime fiction, Section 2 examines recent crime fiction that not only includes multiple perspectives from the adoption triad – hence, expanding the single adoption story – but also complicates, challenges, and revises traditional notions of the crime/detective formula story. This section centers stories and plotlines from marginalized members of the adoption triad to comment on how intersectional differences of race/gender/nationality/sexuality reveal the ongoing problems behind transracial adoption. By flipping the script, authors like J. S. Lee, Sheena Kamal, Celeste Ng, Jean Kwok, Charmaine Wilkerson, S. A. Cosby, Walter Mosley, and Lynn Liao Butler offer alternative perspectives and possibilities of adoption as a practice of survival, self- and community-centered empowerment, and acceptance.

Section 3 examines the role of DNA and the search process in adoption crime fiction. With the popularization of DNA and ancestry kits, accessing information to unknown blood relatives has never been easier. But, what does DNA do and not do? By looking at stories like Dani Shapiro's *Inheritance* (2019), which reveal how DNA can shatter people's identities and reveal long-held family secrets as well as examining the business of DNA in popular culture, this section explores the search process in adoption crime narratives. In adoption narratives, search for biological kin is what literary critic and Korean American adoptee Jenny Heijun Wills calls the "ever-present specter" (65) that haunts adoptees'

---

[5] Recent comments by Supreme Court Justice Amy Coney Barrett, a transracial adoptive mother of two adopted children from Haiti, who argued that safe haven laws are a solution to unwanted pregnancy, have been heavily criticized by both reproductive rights and adoption advocates. See Phelan and Briggs's "Making."

search for identity. Furthermore, like the detective plot at the center of mysteries, the search plot is, according to critic Barbara Melosh, what has "captured the imagination of a larger public" (227). But, unlike the typical mystery story where reaching the solution (the "whodunit") is the goal, adoption searches are often left with questions unanswered.

Finally, the Coda concludes with a personal reflection on Susan Kiyo Ito's new memoir *I Would Meet You Anywhere*. As a transracial adoptive mother whose daughter is about to begin her own search and reunion journey, *Bloodlines* has helped me confront my own insecurities and fears while mothering through adoption as well as a peak into how an adoptee may experience contradictions, frustrations, and solitude in the search/reunion journey.

1 The Fears and Failures of Adoption

Unnerving Headlines: Adoption as Stigma

According to Adoption.com, there are eight misleading stigmas associated with adoption: (1) the "real" effect (or "real" = biological), (2) birthparents give away their children, (3) open adoption is bad, (4) adoption is easy/"just" adopt, (5) adoption is expensive, (6) adoption is second best, (7) birthmothers do not really care for their unplanned pregnancies and, thus, do not keep up with prenatal care, and (8) only rich, White, straight, married couples adopt (Schultz). What this Element targeting potential adoptive parents do not reveal is how these and additional stigmas create a speculative field of nightmare scenarios for the adoption community. Recent headlines highlight and perpetuate these horror stories, weaving "crime" with "adoption" in seemingly inseparable ways. In short, these headlines suggest the impossibility of happy adoptive families.

When Kristine and Michael Barnett adopted Natalia in 2010, they believed she was a six-year-old girl from Ukraine who had a rare bone disorder that caused dwarfism. But, the Barnetts soon came to doubt Natalia's age and accused her of being an adult impersonating a child. The Barnetts accused Natalia of threatening to stab and poison them, declaring "we are living with a con artist sociopath" (Vargas). Medical reports were contradictory: a doctor told the Barnetts that Natalia was an adult, while a local children's hospital concluded she was eleven years old from a skeletal survey. In response, the Barnetts changed her legal age to twenty-two and rented an apartment for Natalia where she would live alone. Meanwhile, the Barnett family relocated to Canada and ceased communication with Natalia. Although the Barnetts were charged with neglect, they were both acquitted of all charges in 2022. The documentary *The Curious Case of Natalia Grace* began streaming on the Discovery Channel in 2023 (Haasch).

When adoptive parents Trezell and Jacqueline West reported their sons, Orrin (4) and Orson (3), missing on December 2020, investigators eventually concluded both boys died three months prior to the missing report. After an extensive investigation that included testimony from the West's eldest child (they have six children total, four adopted and two biological), prosecutors charged the Wests with secondary murder and child cruelty. In May 2023, jurors found the Wests guilty. According to Prosecutor Eric Smith, the Wests were abusive to their adopted children (Kotowski). The bodies of Orrin and Orson have yet to be found.

One of the biggest anxieties potential adoptive parents have is uncovering the child's past history, including medical as well as any history of abuse or neglect. When San Diego couple Sharon and Keith Kramer adopted three-year-old Paul in 1981, they fell in love with his angelic face. Not long after the adoption, however, young Paul began showing increasingly aggressive and harmful behavior such as strangling a neighbor's baby, putting a knife to his neck and threatening suicide, and attempting to molest an eight-year-old girl at age sixteen. The Kramers eventually discovered Paul had fetal alcohol syndrome, a condition that was never revealed to them during their adoption process. With his behavior worsening each year, Paul was eventually institutionalized, which the Kramers could not financially support. The Kramers sued state adoption officials stating that they should have been informed of the birthmother's medical history prior to adoption ("Adoption Nightmare"). Controversial cases like the Kramers highlight the need for full disclosure of the birthmother's and child's health histories, an ongoing legal battle in most of the U.S. states.

Recent legal conundrums have also shed light on how unethical adoption practices have neglected to center children's well-being. A particularly astonishing example is that of 41-year-old adoptee Adam Crapser, who, upon burglary and illegal possession of a firearm convictions, was deported to South Korea because his adoptive parents never filed citizenship papers for him at the time of adoption, placing him in stateless limbo ("Adoptee"). Crapser's life story is especially heart-wrenching when it was revealed that his first adoptive parents relinquished him and the second adoptive parents physically and sexually abused him and his other adopted siblings. The practice of returning adoptees is not uncommon. Disturbing stories of second-chance adoptions or rehoming adoptees where adoptive parents return the child back to adoption agencies and/or re-home them through an underground internet market such as Yahoo or Facebook have recently come to light (Twohey). According to Jenn Morson of *The Atlantic*, approximately 1–5 percent of U.S. adoptions are legally "dissolved" each year. The majority of these adoptions are children of color. Not surprisingly, adoption dissolutions "carr[y] a significant risk of trauma to the child" (Morson).

If these headlines do not instill enough anxiety, trepidation, and frustration for (potential) members of the adoption triad, representations of adoption within fiction, especially crime fiction, emphasize how adoption and crime are indivisibly linked in the popular imagination. The following illustrates some common themes in adoption crime stories, including family secrets that lead to murder, intrusive birthmothers, kidnapped and trafficked babies, and rehoming adoptees that reflect some leading adoption stigmas-turned-nightmares.

The Mystery of Adoption

There is no one singular way adoption as a literary device is incorporated into crime fiction. But, it may be surprising to some just how prevalent the trope of adoption and crime intersect in fiction, specifically how adoption is a mystery often tainted by criminal elements. Even in stories like Laraine Hutcherson's *The Boy Detective and the Mystery of Adoption* (2014), an illustrated book designed for seven- to nine-year-olds, adoption is a mystery that must be solved. A young boy transforms into a mini Sherlock Holmes, deerstalker hat included, when he declares that "[s]trange things are afoot" (Hutcherson) when baby supplies begin to appear. In his quest, the boy questions where babies come from (the store? the sky? the dryer?) and is finally told by his mother about an upcoming baby sister:

> How babies begin with a mom and a dad. But it's not always happy.
> Sometimes it is sad. And sometimes the homes where these babies are
> born, are not working right. They're too broken or torn. These babies need
> places to grow and to thrive, with families to love them and stand by their
> side. (Hutcherson)

As an adoptive mother, Hutcherson presumably wrote this story for potential siblings of adoptees, demystifying adoption for children. The message here is clear: families are heteronormative, birthparent homes are broken, and birthfamilies presumably do not love the relinquished child. Here, adoption-as-mystery is codified even for the youngest readers.

Of course, adoption and crime is not a uniquely North American trope. Although it is the focused area of this particular study, it is important to recognize non-U.S. authors' literary grappling with adoption anxieties. Mystery trailblazers such as Agatha Christie, Margery Allingham, and PD James reveal common adoption insecurities and anxieties. Agatha Christie's *Ordeal by Innocence* (1958), for instance, tells of the murder of Rachel Argyle, wife and mother of five adopted children. Her adopted son Jacko is imprisoned for her murder and dies in prison. Although his "innocence" is ultimately revealed (he convinces his lover to kill his mother), the real story behind the murder mystery highlights questions of kinship and belonging often at the center of adoption. As literary critic Claudia Nelson writes, Rachel Argyle, compensating for her infertility-as-disability, smothers her adopted children, which, in turn, damages them. Birthmothers are criminalized (they are prostitutes, nymphomaniacs, and generally fallen women) and adoptees are social outcasts prone to criminality (Nelson). Margery Allingham's *The China Governess* (1962) reveals fears of the nature-versus-nurture question and anxieties of not knowing your origins. Timothy Kinnit wants to marry the beautiful heiress Julia but her father demands he uncover his adopted lineage. What Timothy learns is that he was abandoned as a baby during wartime evacuation. Could he escape the pre-war slum of Turk Street Mile, the "wickedest street in London" (3)? PD James's *Innocent Blood* (1980) furthers anxieties of adoption by villainizing birthparents, members of the adoption triad often ignored in adoption portrayals. As adoptee Phillippa Palfrey discovers in her search for her biological parents, she was given up for adoption because her parents are imprisoned for the rape and murder of a little girl. James's novel is an adoptee search narrative and a parallel revenge plot by the murdered girl's father that warns and discourages adoptees from digging into their past. All three novels mirror the historical anxieties of adoption in the twentieth century culminating with murderous adoptees and birthparents. For these mystery greats, the real fear of welcoming a stranger into your family is not knowing where they really come from with potential dangers hiding within their genes. While I return to these same genetic concerns in Section 3. where twenty-first-century DNA technologies become detective tools, below are more recently published works that perpetuate these anxieties, highlighting the risks, perils, and traumas of adoption with particular focus on its effects on adoptees and birthmothers.

Family Secrets and "Real" Parents

A common theme in adoption narratives is the discovery of one's own adoption. When Sharon McCone's father passes, she discovers her adoption papers, uncovering the lies she had been told for over forty years. Thus begins private investigator McCone's inquiry into her personal history in Marcia Muller's *Listen to the Silence* (2000), the twentieth McCone novel. To date, Muller has published thirty-five Sharon McCone mysteries which began in 1977 as well as four other mystery series, anthologies, a guide to mystery writing, and a standalone novel co-written with her spouse, acclaimed mystery author Bill

Pronzini. Muller is a living legend in American mystery fiction and was awarded the Mystery Writers of America Edgar Grand Masters Award in 2005 as well as the Shamus Award for Best P.I. in 2010.

While *Listen to the Silence* begins with an adoptee's anguish over discovering the secrecy of her adoption, McCone's search journey introduces a Native-centered perspective on kinship and connection that clarifies the true meaning of family. After discovery, McCone questions whether her family members are still her family. "*Was* he still my brother, or had the discovery of that document nullified the relationship" (34 emphasis in original)? After learning that she is half Shoshone rather than the one-eighth she was led to believe, McCone travels to Flathead Reservation in search of her birthparents. She learns of corruption and murder but, most importantly, learns about the meaning of family. When McCone questions Elwood Farmer about her birth history, he distinguishes Native vs. White kinship formations:

> Our familial relationships aren't as clear-cut as whites', or as formal ... There's been so much mixing among the tribes, and other ethnic groups as well, that those connections are very difficult to sort out. If you and Will want to be related, then you should consider yourselves so. (88)

To McCone, this informal kinship formation produces a "startling and some-what alarming array of possibilities ... [that] by virtue of blood, any number of people might be able to lay claim to me" (88). Even with these possibilities and McCone's eventual discovery of her birthparents, she, alongside her birth-mother, ultimately comes to the conclusion that her "real mother is the woman who raised [her]" (271) and that sometimes birthparents must choose relinquishment in order to keep their children safe.

The family secret behind Lisa Gardner's *The Other Daughter* (2012) centers on a serial killer, adultery, and fraud. Melanie Stokes is the adopted daughter of Patricia and Dr. Harper Stokes, a wealthy couple grieving the violent death of their four-year-old daughter, Meagan. When nine-year-old Melanie is abandoned at Dr. Stokes's hospital several years after Meagan's death, they adopt her as a "substitute daughter" (264). Aware of their daughter's death, Melanie is fully mindful of her tenuous identity as the adopted child:

> In spite of what people like to say, families with adopted children have different dynamics. The beginning was not natural or smooth, but held a closer analogy to dating – everyone wore their nicest clothes, practiced their best manners, and tried not to do anything that would make them look too foolish. Then came the honeymoon phase, when parent and child could do no wrong, since everyone was just so gosh darn happy to have one another. Then, if the adoption was successful, the family finally eased into the

fifty-years-of-marriage stage. Comfortable, well-adapted, knowing each family member's strengths and weaknesses, and loving them anyway. (73)

Melanie's relationship to her adoption is further questioned when a reporter reveals his theory that she is the daughter of a serial killer who was executed for the gruesome death of several little girls. In searching to uncover her family's secrets, Melanie (with the help of FBI agent David Riggs) learns that she is, after all, the daughter of Patricia and her godfather, Jamie O'Donnell. Because of his jealousy and greed for money, Dr. Harper had deceptively plotted to fake Meagan's death in order to access her one-million dollar life insurance money and return her into the family years later as "Melanie" via adoption.

Babies for Sale

Sometimes, it is the external factors and not the intra-familial secrets and corruption that highlight how adoption can destroy families. Edgar Award winner and former president of the Mystery Writers of America Lisa Scottoline is known for her two legal thriller series (Rosato & Associates and Rosato &DiNunzio) as well as several standalone thrillers, historical fiction, and humorous nonfiction. *Look Again* (2009) is a standalone thriller that fictionalizes the adoptive parents' worst nightmare with a plot centering on child kidnapping, murder, and a possible adoption reversal. When investigative journalist Ellen Gleeson glimpses a "Have You Seen This Child?" flyer, she is unnerved by the child's physical similarity to her own adopted three-year-old son, Will. Through her investigations, Ellen discovers a connection between Will, the purported birthmother, Amy Martin, who dies from a suspicious overdose, and the wealthy Floridian socialites, Carol and Bill Braverman, who are offering a million-dollar ransom for their missing son, Timothy. In the plot's climax, Ellen learns that Carol Braverman has schemed with Amy's boyfriend, Rob Moore, to kidnap her son in order to secretly gain access to the ransom in order to pay off her gambling debts. By the end, Carol is murdered by the boyfriend. But, the shocking revelation is that via DNA testing Bill Braverman is not the biological father of Will/Timothy, therefore annulling any legal right he may have to obtain custody of the child. In the end, with birthmother dead, the birthfather criminalized and dead (Ellen realizes that Moore must have been the father), and the socialite husband's paternity negated, Ellen remains the legal parent of Will. Although *Look Again* imagines a nightmare scenario behind adoption, it concludes with the child happily remaining with the adoptive mother.

Young Adult author C. C. Hunter also imagines a child kidnapping behind the adoption of Chloe Holden aka Emily Fuller in *In Another Life* (2019). When

Cash Colton runs into Chloe, he is shocked to see her similarity to the time-progressed image of his foster parents' long-lost daughter, Emily, who was kidnapped at three years old. Cash recognizes Chloe's eerie similarities with Emily and decides to investigate the adoption agency that processed the adoption. It is soon revealed that the agency built its success via kidnapped children from Mexico and Central America. When the baby the Holdens were originally supposed to adopt died suddenly, the agency director switched out the baby with kidnapped Chloe/Emily. Upon uncovering the kidnapping history, Chloe/Emily must reconcile her identity. In the end, both adoptive and biological families remain in Chloe/Emily's life when she declares that "a person loves with their heart, and you don't have to be in someone's belly to be in their heart" (324).

Although child trafficking and corrupt adoption practices are behind many of the adoptees who attend Heritage Camp in Jennifer Hanlon Wilde's *Finding the Vein* (2021), the real culprit of camp counselor and adoptee Paul Anderson's murder is revealed to be an adoptive mother desperate to keep her child safe. When Paul urges Genevieve, the camp nurse, to tell her daughter about her kidnapped past and her birthmother's search for her, Genevieve plots to kill him via anaphylactic shock in order to prevent the secret from ever being revealed. While Genevieve attempts to keep her daughter's birthmother hidden, another storyline is revealed where a birthmother searches for her stolen son (Paul, unbeknownst to him). Tanya Miller is the camp's therapist who specializes in adoption. When she is confronted by two campers-playing-amateur detectives, she reveals her history of enslavement in a baby factory in Thailand. With the help of a Thai nurse, she escaped to a refugee camp and eventually met and married an American man through an online service. In the States, she studied to be an international adoption expert for the sole purpose of reuniting with her son. In short, *Finding the Vein* is a story of two mothers – one adoptive, one birthmother – who desperately cling to their child. Interestingly, Wilde is a nurse practitioner and a transracial adoptive mother of three. At the end of the novel, Wilde clarifies her thoughts on international adoption and the intersection of adoption, crime, and loss:

> International adoption is a complicated issue, and people have intense feelings about it … It is true that kids do better in foster and adoptive families than they do in institutions such as orphanages, where many children languish when there is no social safety net. It is also true that every international adoption starts from a place of sadness and primal loss with the separation of a parent and child. If we ignore either of these issues, we do a disservice to every member of the adoption triad: birth parent, child, and adoptive parent … adoption only happens when something tragic has occurred: a child losing their birth family because of death, severe poverty, illness, or

abuse. Most adoptive families don't want to even consider the possibility that crime and corruption could be part of the process, but it has happened. (219–220)

Thus, Wilde's novel has a dual function. First, it gives voice to both birth-mothers and adoptive mothers who struggle with the consequences of child trafficking that have damaged their and their children's lives. Second, the novel also functions as a warning to adopters to acknowledge that all adoptions *begin with* trauma and loss. To ignore this reality is to ignore the child's history and grief.

Carolyn Wheat's *Fresh Kills* (1995) depicts an adoption world controlled by greedy birthmothers, manipulative doctors and attorneys, and obsessed adop-tive parents who kill in order to protect their family. Wheat, a former defense attorney for the Legal Aid Society in Brooklyn, New York, is a multi-award-winning author (Anthony, Agnes, Shamus, and Mccavity Awards) of the Cass Jameson legal mystery series, of which two are Edgar Award nominees. In *Fresh Kills*, attorney Cass Jameson is cajoled by a fellow adoption attorney to represent a birthmother, Amber, on her impending adoption. The adoption quickly turns sour when Amber, soon after giving birth, changes her mind and decides to keep Baby Adam. Soon thereafter, Amber and her recently wedded husband, Scott, are found murdered. As Cass unfolds the mystery of Amber's death and searches for the missing baby, she discovers a private baby market industry run by a doctor, the adoption attorney that approaches Jameson, and the caregiver of an unwed mothers' home. Jameson quickly learns that Amber has been acquiring money from multiple potential adoptive parents and is eventu-ally killed by the adoptive father of Amber's daughter relinquished five years prior. The most impactful message of *Fresh Kills* centers on the ethics of adoption practices and its privileging of whiteness:

> Do you realize . . . that adoption agencies in the U.S. discriminate in ways the local McDonald's would get sued for? That in an adoption it's not only permissible but required to classify people on the basis of race, age, and religion? . . . It used to be that white couples could adopt nonwhite babies, but now there's a big emphasis put on same-race adoptions. Which leaves a huge number of nonwhite children without homes while white babies are at a premium . . . They even try to match skin color among nonwhite families . . . As if a dark family shouldn't raise a light child. (39–40)

Later, social worker Mickey emphasizes how our governing institutions (health-care, insurance) prioritize supporting biology and whiteness:

> Look at the way we pay for babies. I'll bet every visit your Ellie Greenspan [the potential adoptive mother] made to a fertility specialist was covered by

insurance. But no one pays for the cost of adoption. Which is society's way of saying that if you choose to reproduce yourself, in spite of all the children already born who need homes, we'll subsidize you. And if you can't have your own, we'll help you find a white infant if you're the right age, the right religion, live in the right place, and have lots of money . . . And in a capitalist society, we therefore justify the creation of science of white babies and the sale of white babies by birth mothers. (41)

Fresh Kills shows how the desire for a child can become a commodified obsession that is also governed by and reflective of our cultural priorities of biology and race. It also shows how the maintenance of White family formations is supported, nurtured, and institutionalized by healthcare and insurance industries and governmental policies.

One of the nation's leading adoption attorneys, Randall Hicks is also the author of both parenting and adoption books (his bestseller *Adopting in America: How to Adopt Within One Year* is in its sixth edition) and a mystery series featuring Toby Dillon, adoption attorney and tennis coach-turned-detective. The second novel in the series, *Baby Crimes* (2007), begins when a wealthy couple is blackmailed over the illegal adoption of their daughter sixteen years ago. They suspect the birthmother is behind the blackmail and hire Dillon to find her and make the adoption retroactively legal. Through twists and turns, Dillon discovers a crime syndicate that kidnaps children for trafficking. The crime boss declares, "[T]hey're a cash crop, my friend. Used to be we went with teenagers. Runaways mostly. Nobody missed 'em. But nowadays, it's the little ones the pervs want. Train 'em early so they grow assuming it's the way everybody lives. Ya know? Ship 'em out of the country and they never see the light of day again" (200). But, we learn at the end that the blackmail letters were sent by the adopted child in order to force her parents to be honest and upfront about her adoption. In short, *Baby Crimes* is a story of a girl who wants transparency and honesty from her adopted parents about her adoption.

Not all child kidnapping occur due to large child trafficking syndicates, however. Helen Klein Ross's *What Was Mine* (2016) is a story of a desperate woman, Lucy Wakefield, who kidnaps a baby and raises the child for twenty-one years. Lucy and her husband, Warren, are an average American couple: White, middle-class, professional. But after years of struggling with infertility and Warren refusing to adopt because "he didn't want to inherit someone else's problems" (7), Lucy's desperation for motherhood does not cease, leading to the ultimate demise of her marriage. Alone and despondent, Lucy discovers a baby left alone in a shopping cart one day and, in the spur of the moment, takes her. Surprisingly, before the advent of the internet in the 1990s, Lucy gets away with the kidnapping and raises baby Mia for the next twenty-one years. It is when Lucy writes a book about a kidnapped baby that she is confronted by Mia's birthmother, Marilyn, who recognizes the story. Although the premise of Ross's novel centers on the kidnapping, the second half of the novel focuses on the "real" dilemma (real families, real mothers). The language of "real" is a common struggle for adoptees and we see Mia coming to terms with this as she is reunited with her birthmother and half-siblings.

> When I walked into [Marilyn's] house, I burst into tears. When you grow up in a family that isn't your birth family, sometimes you feel you're not actually real. Because you don't see yourself reflected in anyone else around you. Now, suddenly, I was among people who looked like they'd been made from the same clay. (217)

For Mia, "real" is the similarity due to biology. It is this similarity that results in a bond and familiarity that becomes the foundation to their relationship. Marilyn, too, turns to biology to create a connection between mother and child. "A true mother can't ever distance herself from a body that began in her own" (286). On the other hand, Lucy realizes that experience and the act of mothering throughout the years is what defines a mother. When she comes across another baby left alone in IKEA, she realizes the "monstrousness of what [she] had done. Now [she] would never be capable of it. Because [she has] a child. [She] know[s] what the stakes are" (274). By the end of the novel, Mia comprehends the struggle of the "real" question when she says, "I have my birth mother. But I miss my mom" (288). The final scene shows Mia reuniting with her mother, Lucy.

Birthmothers: From Possibilities to Nightmares

In addition to child trafficking, one of the biggest concerns in adoption is the role of the birthmother/birthfamilies and the degree of openness between the two families. Do you want an open adoption? If so, how much should the birthmother play a role? When Molly Arnette begins the adoption process after a hysterectomy, it also evokes her childhood trauma of her father's death. Through alternating chapter timelines between Molly's present in San Diego and her childhood past in North Carolina, we learn how adoption is already very much a part of Molly's identity. In part, Diane Chamberlain's *Pretending to Dance* (2015) is a story about how adopted families can successfully incorporate both birthmothers and adoptive parents in an inclusive, open household. Molly's navigation of the adoption process and the challenges of how best to support the birthmother while clarifying boundaries forces her to come to terms with her own unique childhood. When we see Molly as a teenager, we learn that she lives in a family compound, Morrison Ridge, that includes her parents, aunts and uncles, grandmother, and biological mother. When Molly was two years old, her birthmother, Amalia, arrived at Morrison Ridge overwhelmed and unable to mother her child. By then, Molly's father was married and had just been diagnosed with multiple sclerosis. He agreed to raise Molly and insisted Amalia live nearby to be close to their child. His wife, Nora, adopted Molly and raised her like her own.

The mystery and crime of the novel are introduced early on, but we don't learn the truth until the very end alongside Molly. "My mother murdered my father" (7) is the secret that Molly has been holding on to since her father's death. Since then, Molly believed Nora poisoned her deteriorating, disabled father. Angry and in grief, Molly abandons Morrison Ridge and her family for the next twenty years. It is not until she returns to Morrison Ridge in the present that she discovers her father's death was an act of assisted suicide committed by his beloved community, including family members, coworkers, and friends. In a scene reminiscent of Agatha Christie's *Murder on the Orient Express*, this decision was enacted not out of revenge but out of love. "We all agreed to help someone we loved escape from a life he could no longer bear" (307). Molly reunites with Nora upon learning the truth and with each "baring [their] souls" (318) reveal their individual anxieties of being an adoptee and adoptive mother. "I sometimes worried you didn't love me very much ... I worried it was because I wasn't yours – biologically – and that I might feel the same way about the baby we're" [about to adopt] (318). After Nora confirms her genuine love, Molly returns to San Diego and successfully adopts a daughter. Molly's own identity as an adoptee helps her to acknowledge the birthmother's trauma. "Our very best day had been Sienna's [the birthmother's] very worst. I will never forget that. I know there is still grief inside her. There is grief, but not regret" (335). In a rare glimpse in adoption stories, Chamberlain's novel includes both the recognition of birthmother trauma and the possibility of successful open adoptions.

Chamberlain's *Pretending to Dance* illustrates a successful and rare open adoption story. But alongside headlines like "A Teen Reunited with Her Birth Mother Who Then Killed Her" (Selk), Minka Kent's *The Memory Watcher* (2017) poses a less-than-ideal adoption scenario where the birthmother is vilified as psychotic and the adoptive mother adopts for less-than-ideal maternal reasons. Readers are immediately introduced to Autumn Carpenter, a birthmother who gave up her baby girl when she gave birth at fifteen. Years later, unable to forget her daughter, Carpenter finds her daughter's adoptive family via the mother's social media account. Carpenter becomes obsessed with this family, and when the account suddenly disappears one day, she maneuvers a way to become a part of the family's life. As their summer nanny, Carpenter is able to witness the family from the inside out. What she discovers is less than ideal. The father, Graham McMullen, is having an affair and the mother, Daphne McMullen, turns to drugs and an affair with her drug dealer. It turns out that Carpenter's boyfriend's sister, Marnie, is Graham's lover. When she is found dead, both Mr. McMullen and Carpenter are suspects. But, it is ultimately revealed that Mrs. McMullen ordered the hit to get rid of her nemesis. In a twist at the end, Carpenter is also revealed to actually be Sarah Thomas, a psychiatric patient who disappeared from her abusive family. As a patient, she befriends the real Autumn Carpenter and eventually kills her and takes over her identity. Kent reveals that the story was born during her own infertility struggles and preoccupation with online mommy blogs. There, she fell in love with one particular family and their "beautiful, dreamy little life" (viii). When the account suddenly disappeared one day, similar to Carpenter's experience with @MeetTheMcMullens above, Kent realized the "wake-up call" (viii) of immersing oneself into online fantasies at the risk of living her own life. Thus, *The Memory Watcher* may caution against fabricated online personas but it also maintains the image of the unhinged birthmother and the self-absorbed adoptive mother who doesn't actually want to be a mother.

The troubling representation of the unhinged birthmother and the incapable adoptive mother is again portrayed in Jenna Kernan's *The Adoption* (2022). *The Adoption* begins with Dani Sutton being released from a psychiatric facility. She is recovering from a car accident which disabled her sister, Shelby, and left herself with a brain injury and condition called acquired prosopagnosia or face blindness. Dani is unable to recognize faces and must rely on people's other distinguishing markers like clothing, voices, or unique physical indicators (gait, scars, etc.). Dani's husband, Judge Tate Sutton, is an ambitious politician and desires a seat in the Florida Supreme Court. Dani nervously returns home and adjusts to her new home, a McMansion Tate had purchased shortly before her accident. Dani gets reacquainted with her neighbors, including Enid, who lives across the street and is going through an ugly divorce. Although Dani is unable to have children due to the accident, she fantasizes about filling up their large home with children until, one day, Tate announces that not only are they approved for adoption but have been chosen by a birthmother. Dani is surprised since their previous attempt was denied due to her medical condition. She suspects Tate must have done something illegally but quickly pushes that suspicion aside when she meets her new baby, Willow. Dani quickly falls into mother mode when a strange woman appears outside her home. Because of her face blindness, Dani is unable to recognize this person. When a woman confronts her again at a doctor's office, Tate questions her sanity. At the climax of the story, Dani is confronted by her psychiatrist, Dr. Allen, and Tate, who reveal to her that her sister's horrific death at the accident forced Dani to forget the trauma, requiring her hospitalization for not six months as she thought but six years. During that time, Tate had an affair with Enid who got pregnant. Their scheme was to have Dani adopt the baby in order for Tate to still have access to her inheritance. When Dani suspects something is wrong with the adoption, Tate tells her that Willow was actually born via a surrogate and is biologically Dani and Tate's baby. But, Enid is the jealous other woman and also a birthmother and begins harassing Dani. Eventually, Enid's estranged husband attacks Tate, leaving Dani to believe he is dead. In a final plot twist, Dani, a recovered Tate, and the police scheme to have Enid confess to her role in her husband's attack against Tate. In the end, Willow remains with Tate and Dani's adoption is revoked while she remains hospitalized.

If Kent's story fails to caution against haunting and intrusive birthmothers, A. M. Homes's *In A Country of Mothers* (1993) offers another perspective on how adoption relinquishment plagues birthmothers. Homes's novel centers on a therapist, Claire Roth, and her relationship with her young patient, Jody Goodman. It turns out that young Claire was forced by her parents to relinquish her baby under questionable and mysterious circumstances. "It's better this way" (45), Claire's mother tells her. But when Jody becomes a new patient and reveals that she is an adoptee, Claire's perfect life is threatened. "Claire had worked hard to make herself this life, this marriage, these children, and now she suspected that she'd done all this as a cover-up, so no one would notice she was a fraud. She lived in fear of being discovered" (43). Their relationship as patient and therapist quickly becomes blurred when they become co-dependent on each other. Claire suspects Jody is her long-lost daughter and "speculation turns into certainty, fantasy into fixation" (book cover). Jody's adoption is also questioned when she discloses that her parents turned to adoption shortly after the death of their only child. As a replacement child, Jody struggles with her identity, seeing her dead brother as a "ghost" (64). "I am him, he is me" (64), she tells Claire. What makes this story particularly memorable is Homes's own identity as an adoptee and her struggles when ultimately reunited with her birthparents. In her 2007 memoir titled *The Mistress's Daughter*, Homes reveals what happened when, at age thirty-one, her birthparents found her, forcing her to disentangle fantasy from reality (see Section 3 for more on Homes's memoir).

The role of birthmothers becomes further complicated when surrogacy takes place as a form of adoption. Toni Halleen's *The Surrogate* (2021) describes the legal, emotional, and cultural turmoil of using surrogacy as a path to mother/parenthood. Ruth Olson is recently married to Hal Olson, a divorced father of two teenage sons. Ruth longs to have a child with Hal, to be "someone's mom ... and to be inside a microsphere ... with Hal" (66) as he is with his ex-wife and sons. But, Ruth's path to motherhood is ambiguous due to her use of a surrogate. This is particularly telling when at the hospital during the child's birth. As intended parents but not the woman giving birth, the hospital staff are unsure how to treat Ruth, including allowing her to stay overnight as well as abiding by their birth plan. The nurse's lack of consideration for the intended mother becomes clear during a breastfeeding scene where she coaches Cally how to nurse amidst Ruth's reminder that this goes against the birth plan.

> This had been a sore spot for Ruth. She believed that, as the intended mother, she'd experienced second-class treatment and an undercurrent of disapproval at many of the stages of the process. She'd complained to me at night about the way the nurses stared at her, like she was, in her words, the freak at the circus. She'd caught them whispering. She felt they didn't view her as the baby's mom. And no matter how much I tried to convince her not to worry about others' opinions, she said she felt like she had a flashing neon sign over her head that said "Infertile – Used a Surrogate." (139)

Completely ignoring Ruth, the nurse replies, "Breastfeeding helps the mother's body ... The sucking triggers the uterus to shrink back" (124). The "crime" occurs when Cally sneaks out of the hospital with the baby. Who the mother is and at what point the intended mother becomes the recognized mother are the questions Halleen's story asks. When Cally sneaks out of the hospital with the baby, the hospital staff tell the Olsons they cannot treat this as a crime because, to them, Cally is the mother to the baby. To make things more complicated, when questions of child support comes up, Hal is shocked to learn he may be responsible because he is the biological father. Ultimately, *The Surrogate* is an unusual adoption crime novel because there is no adoption and there is no crime, per se, due to the surrogate's change of mind. In that sense, Halleen's novel shows the terrifying possibilities of how surrogate adoptions can go bad. In the end, Ruth becomes naturally pregnant and *The Surrogate* functions as a warning to readers against using surrogacy as a solution.

Return to Sender

A phenomenon that is rarely discussed in adoption discussions and perhaps the most tragic is the concept of reactive attachment disorder (RAD) and rehoming adoptees. RAD is the inability to emotionally and psychologically bond between child and parent, usually the mother. RAD may occur when the child does not receive adequate comfort, security, and nurturing as a child. For adoptees or foster children who are not adopted or abused and/or repeatedly transferred from one home to another, RAD is a common consequence. James Grippando's *Gone Again* (2016), the twelfth Jack Swyteck novel and the winner of the 2017 Harper Lee Prize for Legal Fiction, tells the story of how RAD destroys families unable to bond and rehoming, the act of "placing the child with a new family that is better able to provide for her" (151), is sought as a solution. *Gone Again* begins when Sashi Burgette, a young Russian adoptee, disappears and ex-con Dylan Reeves is about to be executed for her death. When Sashi's adopted mother, Debra, seeks criminal defense lawyer Jack Swyteck's help, he uncovers Sashi's troubled background as an orphan in Chechnya and her disturbing non-integration into her adopted life in the U.S. Debra discloses that very little is known about Sashi's background as a result of the Chechen wars with the possibility that she was stolen from her parents. As a psychiatrist tells Swyteck, RAD is a "mental disorder … [which gives a] false belief that he or she is incapable of being loved" (86), resulting in rejecting physical contact and displaying beyond normal acts of manipulation, lying, cheating, and other destructive behaviors. To the Burgettes, Sashi was "beyond any help" (67) and their desperation led to a rehoming "broker" (253) who would find another home for "damaged" (258) Sashi. Ultimately, the rehoming was not successful and Sashi's death was revealed to be at the hands of her adopted father. Grippando's novel of an adoption gone wrong further supports the common unease with adoption, especially international adoption. The lack of access to the adoptee's history destroys the adopting family and reveals just how much adoption can be an industry governed by the fundamental belief that children function as commodity. ""[A]ll it takes [is] a power of attorney" (256), the broker tells Swyteck. Grippando, a former trial attorney, clearly understands that, by a mere signature, adopted children can be tossed and discarded.

Tragically, the fictional story of Sashi as "damaged goods" echoes the very real ways the Hart children described in the Introduction were represented by their adoptive mothers. Prior to adopting the six Hart children, Jennifer and Sarah Hart fostered another young girl who they ultimately abandoned, without warning, at a therapist office, never to be seen again. When Hannah Hart, 15, escaped to her neighbor's home about a year before the murder-suicide, the Hart mothers explained the kids were "drug babies" with a bipolar birthmother in an attempt to explain away Hannah's behavior and missing teeth (see Asgarian). Unfortunately, the line between fiction and reality is too easily blurred here. This section shows the myriad ways adoption is negatively portrayed, often-times perpetuating misrepresentation and silence. We are eager to hear the flip side. Section 2 disrupts this silence by centering BIPOC voices from the adoption triad, especially adoptees. From these perspectives, perhaps we can help the Hart children and others like them shout loud and clear.

2 Beyond the Single Adoption Story

As this Element is being written, the emotional and legal complications surrounding transracial adoption continue to center news headlines. In June of 2023, the Supreme Court upheld the Native American adoption law based on the 1978 Indian Child Welfare Act (ICWA), which prioritizes Native American children remain within Native tribes. Distinguishing between tribal self-governance and race, Native adoption cases bring to the forefront the legal and ethical questions of who can properly raise adopted children across racial lines. When Chad and Jennifer Brackeen, a White couple from Texas, became foster parents to a nine-month-old Native baby boy in 2016, they thought it would be short term. But with both birthparents' parental rights terminated and both of the baby's affiliated Navajo and Cherokee tribes in agreement, the Brackeens were allowed to adopt the boy. But, complications arose when the birthmother had a little baby girl. The Brackeens filed for custody in order to keep the siblings together but the Navajo placed the child with a distant aunt. A state judge gave the Brackeens shared custody, resulting in the case going to the Supreme Court. Is a child better off being raised by her Native community or is it better to keep her together with her biological sibling and the only parents she has known? That Justice Amy Coney Barrett, a transracial adoptive mother who recently questioned the need for abortion when adoption is an option, wrote the majority opinion for the 2023 ruling upholding ICWA adds to the complication behind cases like the Brackeen's (VanSickle).

Section 1 highlights some of the ugly realities of adoption and its discomforting portrayal in fiction. From the depiction of birthmothers as both human incubators and psychotic stalkers to international rings of child traffickers that reveal a thriving baby market industry, it is no wonder that adoption as a cultural practice has had a negative image in popular media and consciousness. Although the realities of our history and maintenance of the baby industrial complex demand attention and resolution (see Briggs, Roberts, Homans, and Trenka), this section takes a slightly different approach in examining adoption and crime. Calls to center adoptee and birthmother/parent voices, especially those from the BIPOC and LGBTQ communities, have been the focus of emerging academic areas such as Critical Adoption Studies (see Homans, "Critical"). The recently published award-winning memoirs by transracial adoptees such as Nicole Chung's *All You Can Ever Know* (2018), Jane Jeong Trenka's *The Language of Blood* (2003) and *Fugitive Visions: An Adoptee's Return to Korea* (2009), Susan Devan Harness's *Bitterroot: A Salish Memoir of Transracial Adoption* (2018), Rebecca Carroll's *Surviving the White Gaze* (2021), and Shannon Gibney's *The Girl I Am, Was, and Never Will Be* (2023) are just a few examples of adoptees exposing their racial isolation alongside the immense grief, loss, and trauma of losing their birth families. Memoirs like these have laid the critical and social justice-centered foundation for this particular study and this particular section.

This section is a small attempt to help remedy the silence of BIPOC voices affiliated with adoption. While the previous section focuses on the criminalization of adoption in practice (foster care, adoption industrial complex, etc.) to cultural and literary representations of adoption, adoptees/foster children, and birthmothers as "criminal," it also demonstrates that perspectives were predominantly focused on White adoptive parents by White authors. Adoptees and birthmothers, particularly those from marginalized backgrounds (race, sexuality, geography), are routinely disregarded. Alongside the current movement to #flipthescript that centers adoptee voices, this section focuses on BIPOC perspectives from each corner of the adoption triad. By re-aligning the adoption story, the nuances and intersectional complexities behind earlier questions of who can/is allowed to parent and what is at stake for contemporary family formations become more urgent.

I recognize that with the exception of two authors studied in this section – Lyn Liao Butler (adoptive mother) and JS Lee (transracial adoptee) – it is unknown if the authors below have a personal connection to and/or experience with adoption. When that connection is publicly known, I include it below. My hope is that those who identify as part of the adoption triad, especially writers from marginalized groups, will author stories from their unique perspectives in order to expand our understandings of how adoption impacts everyday lives and communities. In the meantime, I focus on these contemporary writers of color – many of whom are activists, all of whom have been vocal about experiencing racisms and/or writing about racial justice – who flip the script for each member of the adoption triad. By giving voice to adoptees, birthmothers, and adoptive parents of color, they thoughtfully and critically incorporate adoption into their narrative plot to comment upon racial and gender disparities, assimilation, and the ongoing search for belonging and identity within cultures and borders that continuously seek to further their marginalization. Utilizing the crime and mystery genre, these authors reveal the varied ways adoption and crime intersect, forcing readers to question assumptions about kinship, traditional definitions of crime, and the relationship between ethics and the law.

The Problem with Transracial Adoption

One has only to consider James Patterson's Michael Bennett series to understand how transracial adoption becomes a problematic image. Michael Bennett is a NYC detective who becomes a widow in the first novel, *Step On a Crack* (2007). His wife's death also makes Bennett a single father to his ten multiracial adopted children. Deemed the "Bennett Nation" of Black, Brown, and Asian children, they often stop traffic wherever they go. At Christmas, the Bennett children function as ornaments who exemplify the performative aspect of transracial adoption. Bennett described his wife, Maeve, as having a "thing for the misfortunate and strays" (25) and "instead of antiques and Persian rugs a lot of [their] neighbors seem to be into, Maeve filled our house with children" (35–36). The Bennett Nation, it seems, is a multiracial assemblage of White humanitarianism, salvaged, collected, and displayed.

Transracial adoption as a display of performative White allyship is a common trope in adoption narratives (see Julayne Lee). This is the core problem adoptee Paloma encounters with her White adoptive parents. Amanda Jayatissa's *My Sweet Girl* (2021) reveals the desperate lengths orphans take to get adopted. *My Sweet Girl*, the winner of the ITW Thriller Award for Best First Novel, is a psychological thriller with alternating timelines, one in present-day San Francisco and the other in an orphanage in Ratmalana, Sri Lanka, in 2002. The story centers on two twelve-year-old orphan girls, Lihini and Paloma. Paloma is adopted by a wealthy American missionary couple, Mr. and Mrs. Evans, because Mrs. Evans sees her reading Charlotte Bronte's *Wuthering Heights*, a favorite of her own, while visiting the orphanage. Adopted and growing up in San Francisco, Paloma endures subtle microaggressions living as a Brown woman in a "Clorox-white world" (254). The novel's mystery begins when Paloma discovers her blackmailing roommate dead at the kitchen table. The plot thickens when the dead roommate's body disappears and Paloma struggles with alcohol-induced hallucinations and memory loss, stalking men, pestering neighborhood women, and her parents' recent decision to cease financial support. We also learn the backstory of Paloma's childhood at the orphanage and the possible source of her guilt. Through it all, we witness how, as a transracial adoptee, Paloma never feels like she fits in. "You just don't look like an Evans" (25), she's told.

Although the foregrounding plot of mystery and crime is the main storyline of *My Sweet Girl* (think switched identities a la Wilkie Collins's *The Woman in White* and a madwoman reminiscent of Charlotte Bronte's *Jane Eyre*), the underlying commentary highlights the adoption industry and White saviorism. When Lihini and Paloma first meet Mr. and Mrs. Evans, it is their fairness that attracts the potential American adopters. Both are, in fact, called *sudhu* by everyone in the orphanage, a term that functions as an endearment highlighting their light skin. When Paloma migrates to San Francisco, she quickly learns that her new parents' adoption of her includes erasing parts of her identity that are not compatible with their aims. For instance, when Paloma suggests they learn Sinhalese, they think she is joking and enroll her in French instead. Or, when Paloma uses coconut oil on her hair, Mrs. Evans responds, "[i]t's just so greasy and gross" (171) and buys her expensive conditioner. One of the first things they do when Paloma arrives to the States is fix her front tooth. "You're an Evans now, Dad said. And an Evans would certainly not have a chipped tooth" (171). Paloma reveals the performative urge behind these changes when she asks her parents to change her name. "Why would you want to change something so beautiful and exotic" (257), they ask. Ironically, Paloma points out, it isn't even a Sri Lankan name. Later, Paloma is made to perform adoption as racial spectacle when she helps her mother at adoption charity events.

> All the book club ladies wanted to know what it was *really* like. Was it terrible? There was no internet, or air-conditioning, and did we even wear shoes? Of course it must have been terrible for you, poor thing. I made extra cash when I told them that we had hand-me-down clothes, and that I had never eaten McDonald's until I came to the US, like that ever even mattered to me. (150)

But, Paloma quickly learns how to navigate her racial identity to her advantage via American racial dynamics:

> I didn't think I had much to go on when it came to looks, not like she does anyway, but I did have the exotic card to play, no matter how much it pained me. I know I'm not supposed to do it that way. I know that we (and I use the term we to mean all of us who have been dealt the shitty hand of having too much melanin in this Clorox-white world) have been through too much, fought too much for our rights, been eroticized and disregarded, for me to use the exotic-brown-girl stereotype to my advantage. I get it. It cheapens our cause. I hate that I have to do it. But fuck you, this is the hand I've been dealt and now you want me not to play the only trump card I've got? (254)

As Paloma assimilates into American culture and her new adopted identity, she quickly learns about American racism towards Black and Brown bodies. Even in the multicultural mecca of San Francisco, Paloma is constantly questioned about her adopted and racialized identity. Strangers are confused with her Anglo-sounding surname and often mistake her for "some other brown chick" (153). "Why does everybody assume that I'm not from here? I know I'm brown, but isn't San Francisco supposed to be a fucking melting pot of cultures? Isn't that what it says on every damn blog post about the place? *San Francisco – the poster child for cultural diversity*" (146). The inability to tell one Brown person from another is emphasized at the climactic conclusion of the novel when we learn that the Evanses failed to realize that Lihini was passing for Paloma all along. *My Sweet Girl* epitomizes the scathing criticism against White saviorism behind transracial adoption. The real crime is the adoption industrial complex that enables wealthy Americans the ability to take children from poorer countries and bleach any sign of difference out of them. As reviewer Rachel Jackson argues, the ending shows that "white humanitarianism . . . requires that chosen recipients be interchangeable, singularly unique, or disappear as needed" (Jackson).

Thrity Umrigar's *Everybody's Son* (2017) is not generally described as crime fiction but its plotline of race and adoption transforms it into a crime story hidden behind White liberal saviorism. The story intersects the troubling and connected corners of the child welfare system (foster care, the court system, and adoption agencies) that routinely separates children from birthfamilies due to race, poverty, mental illness, drug use, disability, and immigration status. Within this landscape, Umrigar's novel problematizes White adoptive parents' personal motivations behind their desire to adopt, blurring the "best interest of the child" rationale that is often touted when children are taken from their biological homes. The plot of *Everybody's Son* is as follows: after the recent death of their son, David and Dolores Coleman decide to adopt Anton, a nine-year-old African American boy whose drug-addicted mother, Juanita, cannot care for him. David Coleman is a prominent liberal Democrat judge with powerful connections who ensures that Juanita has a long prison term. Upon her release, Coleman manipulates her into signing away custody and adopts Anton. With wealth and privilege, Anton thrives by attending Harvard and ultimately becomes attorney general. Anton's rise is interrupted, however, when he eventually discovers how he came to be adopted and reunites with his birthmother at the end. As a crime story, *Everybody's Son* shows that it is a crime to be poor and Black, justifying Juanita's loss of custody. As an adoption story, the novel also shows how the justice system can be easily maneuvered for the wealthy elite. Here, race, class, and power override all individual rights in adoption, especially if those rights belong to the Black and poor.

Similar to *My Sweet Girl*, a core struggle for many transracial adoptees is their navigation of racial identity. For Anton, his confrontation with his blackness occurs while at Harvard when he meets Carine, a vocal Black activist. While at dinner with Anton's parents and former-senator grandfather, Carine passionately condemns American imperialism. With his family's quickening anger and defensiveness, Anton soon realizes that his family's discomfort arises from Carine's blackness:

> And then suddenly, swiftly, he knew – if Carine had been a white girlfriend arguing exactly the same points, they would've indulged her, cast a bemused

eye toward her politics, maybe even admired her sensitivity toward the earth's poor. What're you, a Commie? his father would've teased. It was Carine's skin color, her blackness, that made her suspect. That made them feel there was an alien in their midst, a spy in their own country. (155)

Of course, the family's reactive response toward Carine emphasizes their own imperialist practice behind Anton's very adoption. But, Anton is unaware of this reality at this point in the novel and soon breaks with Carine, believing they are incompatible. She addresses his distance to his racial identity when she tells him, "I can't decide if you're the blackest white man I've ever met or the whitest black man" (156). By the end of the novel, Anton discovers his adoption secret and reunites with both his birthmother and Carine, realizing that "[h]e has never felt this at ease in the world" (335).

The ethical problem presented here which crosses criminal lines is the question of wealthy White elites adopting children of color. Here, the Colemans adopted Anton in order to assuage their grief over their biological son's death which forces us to question whether they really adopted with Anton's best interest in mind. Additionally, the adoption is guided by White paternalism which defines bad (i.e. Black mothering) versus good (White and wealthy) parenting. That Anton eventually reunites with his birthmother and finally feels "at ease" tells us that the search narrative may not only reveal information about the adoptee's genetic family but the search journey also discloses the secrets, silences, and shame kept hidden within adopted families as well.

But not all adoptees are able to reunite with their birthparents and/or discover their origin story. This void could intensify the racial isolation and, at times, result in extreme outcomes. Sherman Alexie's *Indian Killer* (1996) is a story about a serial killer terrorizing and scalping White men in Seattle, Washington. Deemed the "Indian Killer," he ignites incidents of anti-Native violence and hostility. Interspersed with the killer's storyline is a parallel story of John Smith, a Native man adopted by White parents. Smith is desperate to connect with his Native heritage but struggles with mental illness and isolation and has very minimal understanding of his Native identity:

John only knew that he was Indian in the most generic sense. Black hair, brown skin and eyes, high cheekbones, the prominent nose. Tall and muscular, he looked like some cinematic warrior, and constantly intimidated people with his presence. When asked by white people, he said he was Sioux, because that was what they wanted him to be. When asked by Indian people, he said he was Navajo, because that was what he wanted to be. (32)

When he meets Marie, a Native activist, Smith becomes invested in the politics of Native rights. The detective and adoption plots come together to make ambiguous the killer's identity. The title itself – *Indian Killer* – offers two interpretations: a killer who *is* Indian versus a killer *of* Indians, referencing the loss of Native identity through transracial adoption and/or through the co-optation/cultural appropriation of Nativeness through characters like Dr. Clarence Mather, the White colonizing professor, and Jack Wilson, the former Seattle policeman-turned-crime writer with dubious Native ancestry. Thus, Alexie blurs the distinction between actual crime (killing) versus cultural genocide, reminiscent of the 1972 National Association of Black Social Workers condemning transracial adoption as genocide.

American Exceptionalism

As evidenced in Section 1, one of the biggest concerns with adoption, both domestic and transnational, is child trafficking. Jacinda Townsend's *Mother Country* (2022) offers an unusual perspective of a woman who, infertile and longing for motherhood, abducts a child while traveling abroad. *Mother Country*, winner of the 2022 Ernest J. Gaines Award for Literary Excellence, is not categorized as crime fiction per se but a criminal act functions as the plot's climactic moment where readers must make the ethical decision to empathize (or not) with the protagonist. In short, Townsend asks, who has the right to mother? As a crime story, *Mother Country* is a tragic tale of child kidnapping that highlights American exceptionalism prominent in adoption narratives. Shannon is a young African American woman who recently learns she is infertile due to a car accident. Infertile, jobless, and in a marriage of convenience, Shannon describes herself as a "foster child hoping for adoption" (92). She finds security in her new husband, Vlad, and keeps her infertility and debt woes from him. Vlad soon pressures Shannon for a child because it's what "the normal people ... the people who make the future" (107) do. After failed fertility treatments, they embark on a business trip to Marrakech. Here, Shannon wanders through the Medina in Essaouira, a walled-in eighteenth-century town with cafes, galleries, and alleyways lined with shops. During her excursions, Shannon takes interest in a three-year-old girl wandering the marketplace seemingly without parents or adult supervision. After offering her ice-cream and silently naming her Mardi (the girl's name is Yu), Shannon impulsively takes her as her own.

This act of seizing possession may seem outrageous to the reader, revealing Shannon's sense of entitlement and greed. But, perhaps the most disturbing moment throughout this abduction scene is the various descriptions of

Shannon's unknown accomplices. Although Hafiza, the soap stall owner and friend of Souri, Yu's mother, witnesses Shannon taking Yu/Mardi, she does nothing because she believes it is the "divine plan" (189). When Mohammed, the hotel receptionist, sees Shannon accompanying Yu/Mardi to the elevator and doesn't "feel right in [his] gut" (190), he remains silent because he realized "[t]he Americans and the Europeans often had their own strange business . . . and it never profited to care" (190). Although the consulate official, Fouad, initially refuses to sign papers for Vlad and Shannon to take Yu/Mardi to the States, he quickly changes his mind when bribed and blackmailed. When an airport janitor Fatoumata witnesses Yu/Mardi crying at the terminal, she misreads Shannon as her "American auntie, taking her for the vacation of a lifetime" (193). For Vlad, Yu/Mardi is the solution needed to not only secure his marriage but confirm that he is, in actuality, not the bore he always believed he was. Finally, although Shannon recognizes that she has "stolen another woman's child" (210) by coordinating a "new slave transport" (211) of child abduction, she cannot squash her determined need to mother and proceeds.

Interestingly, Shannon's crime is never exposed and Yu/Mardi's adoption is not evident to the external world because of their similar blackness. As Yu/Mardi says,

> No one ever asks, because I'm Black like my parents, and White people rarely find subtlety. They can't see that my skin is toned red where the mom's is toned yellow. They can't see that I look great in blue and the mom does not. They can't see how I'm almost as tall as my parents even though I'm only eight years old, and how that shouldn't, genetically, be the case. My real mother would be able to tell me what colors to wear. She'd tell me how to dress for her height. I'm a girl descended from giants. I bet they know everything about conquering. (250–1)

For Shannon and Yu/Mardi, blackness makes their backstory undetectable to the White gaze. Tragically, by the end of the novel Yu/Mardi realizes the crime and reunites with her birthmother only to learn she has another family by now. They both realize that Yu/Mardi cannot be easily assimilated back into her former life and culture. Although mother and child are reunited, they ultimately decide to live apart and Yu/Mardi returns to the States with Shannon. *Mother Country* shows how the desperate need to mother can lead to extreme, even criminal, measures. If *Mother Country* is designated a crime novel, Shannon would be the criminal who gets away with her crime. But, as an adoption novel that lays out the critical questions of who gets to mother and who determines that right, Shannon gets her happy ending with her child at the book's conclusion. In the end, Shannon recognizes her mistake and knows the "right thing" (288) is to let Yu/Mardi return to her birthmother. Motherhood has, in fact, taught Shannon that loving Yu/Mardi is to let her go. This is her redemption. However, Yu/Mardi also recognizes that she cannot return to her former life and returns to Shannon, realizing that "neither of them had won" (291). The last we see of Souri is her walking down the boardwalk to her husband and child. "They were a family again, sans intrusion" (290).[6]

Flipping the Script: Adoptees

When #flipthescript began as a Twitter hashtag movement in 2014 led by Rosita González at Lost Daughters, an independent collaborative writing project organized by women adoptees, its primary mission was to center adoptee voices:

> #flipthescript sought to create a welcoming space on Twitter for adoptees to express themselves; to reach out to adoptees new to public discourse; to promote acceptance of all adoptee voices as important whether they express happiness, ambivalence, grief and loss, or anger – or all of these themes at once; and to unlabel adoptee narratives as "happy" or "angry" by accepting and expecting complex conclusions from complex life experiences. (TheLostDaughters.com)

This section expands the #flipthescript mission by including birthmother and adoptive parents of color voices to increase the traditional access to adoption and to illustrate how communities of color are changing the adoption landscape. Birthmothers no longer need to hide behind the silencing tactics of shame, gaslighting, and gatekeeping. Birthmother voices bring alternative histories and realities beyond the speculations many adoptees are forced to create. Similarly, adoptive parents of color introduce complexities of family formations and kinship across racial and ethnic borders that force us to examine the assumptions and expectations of what today's family looks like.[7] Finally, adoptees

---

[6] It is interesting to note that Townsend, a former journalist and antitrust lawyer, published an article years before *Mother Country* that called for an urgent need for intraracial adoption. She writes: "The widespread placement of Black children with Whites is an unacceptable solution to current placement needs. Black children deserve to have their sense of identity and community intact. The larger Black community must teach its children how to survive in order to ensure that the Black community itself survives. Efforts are needed not only to keep natural parents with their sons and daughters, but also to find Black adoptive parents when these efforts fail. It is time for the Black community to act, for perhaps the first time in U.S. history, to ensure that only the Black community will control the fate of their Black children" (Townsend, "Re-claiming").

[7] When transracial adoption flips the usual White parent/non-White child image, immediate reactions are often guarded with accusations of crime. As a Black adoptive father of White children, Peter Mutabazi has endured routine calls to the police with allegations of child kidnapping. Today, he carries paperwork to authenticate the adoption wherever he goes. Keia Jones-Baldwin, another Black adoptive parent of a White son, is also routinely accused of kidnapping and also carries adoption papers with her at all times. In another example, Carolyn Sun, an Asian woman married to a White man with a young adopted Black son, is constantly questioned by

highlight how adoption is not just about being grateful (as they are often told to be) but coming to understand, receive, and accept or reject the nuanced and sometimes contradictory realities of their identities. It is only by truly listening to their perspectives can we fully understand how adoption succeeds and fails.

J. S. Lee is an adoptee and author who advocates for adoptee representation. In *Everyone Was Falling* (2020), Lee offers a rare glimpse into a transracial queer adoptee struggling with her own identities while surviving a mass shooting.[8] *Everyone Was Falling* tells the story of Lucy Byrne, a queer Asian adoptee, who returns home for her twentieth high school reunion. Adopted at two and a half years old from South Korea, Lucy is raised by her White parents in a small, predominantly White unnamed U.S. town. The main crime of *Everyone Was Falling* is a mass shooting at the reunion. Lucy and two former high school friends, Christy and Donna, are the only survivors. What is interesting about this crime story is that although the shooter is eventually revealed by the novel's end, the detection of the criminal is not the narrative focus. In fact, for most of the novel, protagonist Lucy is not a very intuitive detective heroine. She mis-detects her ex-husband, Kevin, as the shooter and doesn't follow through on certain observations nor hunches. Furthermore, the shooter's capture is somewhat diminished when he is killed in a bar fight, concluding that particular plot resolution in a disappointing mere paragraph description.

With the absence of a central detective hero(ine), we realize that the novel's real mystery revolves around the racial and sexual dynamics of the three friends – Lucy, Donna, Christy – and, more importantly, around Lucy's survival of a double trauma: the reunion mass shooting and the murder of her mother when Lucy was two and a half years old, resulting in her eventual adoption. These two shootings frame Lucy's ongoing trauma as a transracial adoptee and a double shooting survivor. The real focus of the story, then, is Lucy's self-empowerment of and navigation through her racial, sexual, and adopted identities.

As an Asian adoptee raised by White parents in a small White town, Lucy has been traumatized with her racial isolation. Much of the novel describes Lucy's past and ongoing struggles with family, friends, and coworkers and, in particular, her inability to defend herself. We see that Lucy has been living in a state of ungroundedness where she is constantly being pulled in multiple directions

---

neighbors and professionals such as healthcare workers to verify themselves to be a family. See Mohan, Brown, and Sun.

[8] Additional adoption crime stories from the adoptee perspective include Bharati Mukherjee's *Leave It to Me* (1997), Don Lee's *Country of Origin* (2004), and Sung Woo's *Skin Deep* (2020). For an excellent analysis of Mukherjee and Lee, see Jenny Heijun Wills's "Formulating Kinship" essay.

without an anchor. She's too White and not Asian enough in her non-White community, and her queer identity makes her suspect in the lesbian community. She survives in liminal space without fitting in anywhere. Her inability to detect reflects this unstable identity crisis; she cannot discern her proper place. We also learn that while everyone labels her a "hero" who saved Christy and Donna at the reunion shooting, she rejects that praise by reminding everyone that her quick instincts are a result of her prior experience escaping from another gunfire that killed her mother.

If anything, *Everyone Was Falling* is a primer in contemporary race consciousness and many of its intersectionalities, including White privilege, race passing/colorism, Black-Asian interracial relations, White allyship, White saviorism, BLM versus Blue Lives Matter, White feminism, racial profiling, White fragility, male rage, gun violence, homophobia, and Trump. Very little of the story focuses on the crime until the very end when the shooter is identified as a disgruntled lover. The real detection is Lucy's self-discovery of her own identity. All of the aforementioned "lessons" are what Lucy, as an Asian queer adoptee, has to learn and come to terms with in order to achieve any sense of fulfillment and control. It is only by struggling through the compounded traumas of her intersecting marginalities that Lucy can finally see clearly the shooter's identity. Lee, a Korean adoptee raised in a White community by White adopted parents, writes about the trauma of racial isolation, which resulted in a "fractured identity, experiencing racial confusion and internal bias" (Lee, "The Trauma"). Lee also asks why so many children from war-torn countries are adopted by the very allies that participated in and benefited from those wars.

> The U.S. played a big part in Korea's division, and the Korean War was the catalyst for large-scale international adoption, continuing into my generation and beyond. Intercountry adoption is often political, and connected to the history of transracial adoption within the U.S., which began with colonization, racist policies and cultural genocide against Native and Black peoples. (Lee, "The Trauma")

Similar to criticisms of genocide, transracial adoption is a consequence of war and the politicized, legalized trafficking of children born in its aftermath. In short, adoption and crime is interdependent, reflecting decades of transnational policies and politics that reverberate into intergenerational trauma and loss.

Flipping the Script: Birthmothers

In addition to centering adoptee voices, birthmothers' perspectives and experiences are often overlooked in adoption narratives. Sheena Kamal's Nora Watts series introduces crime audiences to a birthmother as the central protagonist and heroine, a rare depiction in both adoption and literary fiction and creative nonfiction. Nora is a biracial (father is Indigenous and mother is Palestinian) product of Vancouver, Canada's foster care system. Her father committed suicide (later uncovered as murder) and her mother disappeared when she was young, resulting in Nora being placed in multiple foster homes. When we are introduced to Nora in the Macavity and Strand Critics award-winning *The Lost Ones* (2017), we learn that she is the survivor of a brutal rape and attempted murder. When she woke from her six-month coma after the attack, she learned she was pregnant with her assailant's baby and was forced to carry the pregnancy because of Canadian abortion laws. Nora unsuccessfully attempts to self-abort and is institutionalized as a suicide risk after giving up the baby for adoption soon after birth. Since then, Nora has been a homeless alcoholic who now works as an amateur investigator for a small P.I. company. Living on the streets has taught Nora how to rely on and maximize her survival skills of detection and intuition.

> [The peculiar skill I have] is unscientific, though there are plenty out there who claim a scientific knowledge in this field. It's neither Dr. Watson nor Sherlock Holmes. Elementary, maybe, and something a little more than observational. There's a feeling I get when a lie is told. A disgust that creeps up when a liar is doing her best to muck things up or, more likely, save her own ass. Oftentimes, I can't put my finger on it; I can only tell when I see it. And years in foster care honed this skill to an art. (24)

Perhaps in a nod to Tony Hillerman's Leaphorn and Chee Native detective duo, Nora also disregards those who believe she is a natural tracker due to her Indigenous bloodline:

> My heritage is so mixed I wouldn't know where to begin. I would get lost in a forest easier than a tourist with a malfunctioning GPS. I hate the smell of pine and damp earth. Not to mention the various bears, cougars, wolves, coyotes, snakes, spiteful plant organisms, and stinging insects. No woodland romps for me, thank you very much. Give me a dirty street filled with vagrants and littered with needle any day. I know the predators there and they don't bother me anymore. (45)

The first novel, *The Lost Ones* (2017), begins when, Bonnie, the daughter Nora relinquished fifteen years ago, disappears. The adopted parents find Nora in hopes that Bonnie has come looking for her birthmother. As Nora begins to search for Bonnie, we learn that Bonnie's criminal birthfather is looking for his biological daughter in order to cure his dying newborn son via her stem cells. Nora uncovers the "red market," an underground market for human body parts (blood, organs). By the end of the novel, Nora saves Bonnie and they begin a tenuous relationship mostly through text messages and shared photos.

The adoption/reunion subplot gets complicated and interferes with Nora's detection throughout the series. Nora is irritated when outsiders assume her love for Bonnie and denies being her mother but rather is someone who "lent out her womb" (205). Yet, throughout searching for Bonnie and into the series, Nora sporadically admits to herself a connection, albeit tenuous, that she is afraid to consider. Haunting her are questions of who is the "real" mother which is ultimately complicated when the adoptive mother is killed while protecting Bonnie in the series' third novel, *No Going Back* (2020). In the end, Nora realizes she will never have a relationship with Bonnie since Bonnie seemingly rejects her, ultimately questioning the choice to search and reunite.

Often compared to Stieg Larsson's Lisbeth Salander, Nora Watts is a fierce antihero who is deeply troubled from her past trauma and confronts her demons throughout the series, uncovering both illegal crimes (rape, murder, kidnapping) as well as the more hidden crimes that often occur with governmental sanction, questioning how *crime* is, in effect, defined. When Nora learns about Canada's Sixties Scoop, the mid-twentieth-century practice of tearing approximately 20,000 Native children from their families and adopted by White families, she discovers her birthfather's origins. She also learns that many of these children were physically, sexually, and emotionally abused and routinely told they were "bought and paid for, with money handed over to adoption agencies and kickbacks siphoned to crooked government agents" (121). The second novel in the series, *All Falls Down* (2018), is Nora's own search narrative into her veteran Indigenous birthfather who was adopted out to Detroit during the Sixties Scoop. During her discovery, Nora is also shocked to unearth her birthmother who is a Palestinian refugee. By uncovering her birthparents' lives, Nora realizes the intergenerational trauma of loss and longing affecting three generations.

As a crime series, Kamal's Nora Watts series uncovers wealthy Chinese families from abroad, a drug syndicate, corrupt governmental policies in the U.S. and Canada (bribery, tax evasion, immigration), multiple murders, and a kidnapping. We learn that Nora's marginalized identity (as foster child, Indigenous, transient, rape survivor, birthmother) helps instill intuitive detective skills that her male counterparts cannot match. Further, the "why" behind these crimes mostly centers on love and revenge plots such as a father's love for his sick child in *The Lost Ones* or a lover's revenge in *No Going Back* (2020). Throughout the novels, however, the underlying mystery is the secrecy of adoption. Who am I? Where do I come from? Why was I given up? As an adoption series, the novels explore three generations of abandoned or relinquished children searching for their origins and the subsequent effects of these searches. "Wanting to know where you came from doesn't make you weak … but it can make you vulnerable. It can make you crave answers about people you should belong to and places that call to your heart, answers that you're never going to get, from questions you don't have the courage to ask" (255). Perhaps it is through Kamal's award-winning activism and awareness around homelessness that she is able to create a character like Nora Watts, who shows us the vulnerability as a former foster child and birthmother.

Section 1 examines adoption crime stories where birthmothers are portrayed as intrusive, manipulative, and mentally unstable and/or potentially dangerous, justifying the child's adoption and the possible dangers of open adoptions. This section offers an alternative depiction of birthmothers who are often forced to relinquish due to crimes committed against them and/or their lack of resources. These representations show birthmothers loving their children and taking desperate measures, sometimes criminal, to reunite with them. Celeste Ng's *Little Fires Everywhere* (2017), Charmaine Wilkerson's *Black Cake* (2022), and Jean Kwok's *The Leftover Woman* (2023) are three recent birthmother-centered stories that present reasons behind relinquishment that force readers and potential adopters to confront the economic, social, and racial inequities that make children available. Ng's *Little Fires Everywhere* tells parallel stories of four mothers who desperately try to succeed in their mothering. One subplot centers on Bebe Chow, a poor Chinese immigrant abandoned by her husband who, out of utter despair and desperation, relinquishes her baby May Lin at the local fire station. May Lin is eventually adopted by the wealthy McCulloughs who rename her Mirabelle. Bebe tries to get her baby back in court through allegations that the White McCulloughs cannot properly raise Chinese May Lin/Mirabelle. "She's a *Chinese* baby. She's going to grow up not knowing anything about her heritage. How is she going to know who she is" (152 emphasis in original). When the jury awards custody to the McCulloughs, Bebe kidnaps May Lin during the night and returns to China. The question of whether or not Bebe committed a criminal act is ambiguous, however, when Mrs. McCullough is distraught that May Lin did not cry out when Bebe took her, suggesting that the baby knew who her *real* mother was. As a result, the "next baby, [Mrs. McCullough] told herself, coming from an orphanage, would never have known another mother. She would be theirs without question" (331–2). For Mrs. McCullough, babies are interchangeable and fixes her obsessive, entitled need to mother.[9]

---

[9] For an extended analysis of *Little Fires Everywhere*, see my essay "On Mothering."

Charmaine Wilkerson's *Black Cake* (2022) is an intergenerational family saga with secrets of crime (murder, rape, switched identities) and adoption hiding in its core. Coventina (Covey) Lyncook/Eleanor (Elly) Bennett is the biracial (Chinese and Black) protagonist of Wilkerson's novel who flees from her Caribbean island home when she is forced to marry the local criminal money lender Little Man Henry. At their wedding reception, Little Man suddenly dies due to a poisoning. Everyone suspects Covey, especially since she has run off and is never heard from again. Covey escapes to London, where she befriends Eleanor Elly Bennett. Elly was raised in an orphanage and, like Covey, has little family relations. Elly convinces Covey to move to Scotland to pursue better opportunities, but their train crashes and Elly is killed. In a moment of desperation, Covey successfully takes over Elly's identity and begins her new life in Edinburgh. One day, she is raped by her boss and soon learns she is pregnant. Covey/Elly is coerced by nuns at the hostel for unwed mothers to relinquish her baby. The baby, Marble Martin, is adopted by a White couple who keeps the adoption a secret from her. Years later, Covey/Elly learns about many other unwed women who were pressured to relinquish their babies, but is anxious about reaching out to her daughter. The loss of her baby would haunt Covey/Elly until her dying days. Thus, the novel is framed around recordings that Covey/Elly leaves for her son and daughter, Byron and Benny, to disclose her past lives and the news of their unknown sister. By the novel's end, all three siblings are eventually reunited and we learn that Covey's longtime childhood friend, Bunny, poisoned Little Man at the wedding. As an adoption story, *Black Cake* tells the story of a birthmother, the child she surrendered, and an adoption industry that took advantage of disenfranchised women. It also tells of a mother's love for her children near and far.

Jean Kwok's *The Leftover Woman* (2023) is the story of two mothers divided by two countries and cultures but united through the love of a young girl and a government's strict birth-planning policies. When Jasmine gives birth to a girl in China, her husband, Wen, arranges for her adoption to his wealthy White American friends, Rebecca and Brandon, due to China's one child policy and his desires for a son. Jasmine is unaware of this adoption, being told her daughter died soon after birth. But when she discovers an email from the American couple thanking her husband, she hires snakeheads (Chinese mafia that organizes illegal immigration) to bring her to the States. While there, Jasmine becomes her daughter's live-in nanny while also working at an Asian strip club. Her plan is to make enough money to escape with her daughter, Fiona. But her husband eventually discovers where she is, culminating in a confrontation at Rebecca and Brandon's home where Jasmine shoots and kills Wen. Rebecca and Brandon, unaware of Wen's deception and sympathizing with Jasmine's grief, aid Jasmine to avoid legal consequences. In the end, Jasmine realizes she cannot take Fiona away from the only parents she has known. "She does not belong to me. She belong [*sic*] to herself. And the life I want for her, to be safe and loved, I cannot give" (267). Years later, we see Fiona acknowledge that no matter how much her adoptive parents tried, "there was no checklist her parents could tick off that would ever alleviate the grief she felt at being abandoned by her birth parents" (273). The final scene shows Fiona at her birthmother's door, hoping to reunite with the woman who was stolen from her.

Flipping the Script: Adoptive Parents of Color

Another rare perspective in adoption narratives includes adoptive parents of color. The significance of recent portrayals of adoption in Walter Mosley's decades-long and award-winning Easy Rawlins series (1990–2021), S. A. Cosby's *Razorblade Tears* (2021), and Lyn Liao Butler's *Red Thread of Fate* (2022) is about not only expanding the typical representations of the adoption triad (White adoptive parents/non-White adoptees) but also depicting the various pathways to adoption itself. The adoptive parents of color here illustrate that non-White people do adopt, sometimes informally without public acknowledgment, in order to maintain and sustain their communities.

As Grand Master of the Mystery Writers of America and winner of the National Book Foundation Medal for Distinguished Contribution to American Letters, Walter Mosley is a living legend in American literature. Mosley's Ezekial "Easy" Rawlins is arguably one of the most well-known and influential detective figures in detective fiction history. Encompassing fifteen novels in the series thus far (1990–2021), Mosley reveals the ambiguous line between law and justice, racist institutions, centers the distinction between Black survival and White corruption, and routinely demands readers to question the blurred line between right and wrong. As an intellectual (Easy's reading interests include Plato and W. E. B. DuBois), Easy understands how justice does not necessarily comply with Law. For instance, when he discovers that his business partner, Mofass, betrays him in *A Red Death* (1991), he also acknowledges later that he cannot fully punish or judge him because "I hadn't proven to be a better man" (*White Butterfly* 17). We witness Easy's confrontation of right and wrong throughout the series, oftentimes struggling between corrupt White laws and systems and the disenfranchised Black community fighting to survive within those very systems. In addition to solving crimes that often reveal this corruption, we witness Easy's compassion when he adopts Jesus and Feather early on in the series. In *A Red Death*, Easy adopts Jesus, a little Mexican boy he rescues from sexual slavery by an "evil white man" (207) from a previous case. In *White Butterfly* (1992), Easy adopts Feather Starr, a biracial baby whose White prosecutor grandfather kills his daughter, Feather's mother, for having a Black baby. Similar to Easy's own childhood, Jesus and Feather are left abandoned and unloved, without anyone to care for love them. Easy adopts them, finds a respectable job with a pension and health insurance for Jesus and Feather, and navigates the series as a loving and nurturing father. In a society that perpetuates stereotypes that link blackness with criminality, Rawlins's detection demonstrates that it is, in fact, White corruption that is often hidden below the surface and threatens to bleed into the Black community. Throughout his many detections of corruption and greed, Easy also displays that taking care of one's community – in his case, via adoption – is a moral obligation in a world that prioritizes selfish needs and individualistic choices. For Easy, adoption is about taking care of the most vulnerable and disregarded.

On the surface, S. A. Cosby's *New York Times* Bestseller *Razorblade Tears* (2021) is a revenge story of two fathers looking for their sons' killer. But, the underlying story and the killing's motivation make a larger statement about conformity and belonging, particularly around issues of sexuality. The uniqueness of this story lies in the intersections of homophobia/transphobia, racial mixing, and surrogacy/adoption. *Razorblade Tears*, the 2022 Anthony Award winner for Best Novel, is a revenge plot centering on ex-cons Ike Randolph and Buddy Lee Jenkins, Black and White fathers, respectively, who are seeking vengeance for the brutal killings of their gay, married sons, Isiah and Derek, leaving behind their young daughter via surrogacy, Arianna. Both fathers have troubled pasts with their sons, refusing them for their homosexuality. But, when they learn about their sons' deaths, Ike and Buddy Lee partner up and, along the way, come to terms with their homophobia and, for Buddy Lee, his racism as well. We eventually learn that the murders were committed by Derek's stepfather, Gerald, a judge aspiring to be governor, who is confronted by his stepson for having an affair with Tangerine, a transgender woman who has not yet had gender-reassignment surgery. Isiah and Derek are murdered because Gerald, a member of the "first-family-of-Virginia" (94), could not "deal with who [he is]" (309). In the climactic ending, Buddy Lee is shot and he dies. We see Ike finding redemption when he visits Isiah's grave to tell him about their daughter, Arianna, and the lessons he's learned:

> We tell Arianna about you and Derek all the time. We show her the pictures that made it through the fire. We tell her how she's loved by so many people. Me, her grandmothers. Her Aunt Tangerine. Her two guardian angels . . . She won't ever have to wonder if the people who are supposed to love her no matter what actually do. I promise you that. She won't ever have to go

through what you went through. What I put you through ... You know how
you used to say love was love? I didn't get it. I didn't want to get it, I guess.
But, I understand now ... A good father, a good man, loves the people that
love his children. (319)

With the adoption of Arianna, Ike expands his definition of family, masculinity,
and love. The crime behind *Razorblade Tears* is the refusal of non-traditional
love but ends with love, including gay love, transgender love, interracial love,
and non-genetic love.

In Lynn Liao Butler's *Red Thread of Fate* (2022), Tam Kwan is forced
to confront whether or not "love is love" when a tragic accident kills her
husband Tony and his cousin Mia. Almost overnight, Tam becomes
a single mother to the Chinese toddler she and Tony were in the process
of adopting and Mia's five-year-old daughter, Angela. A 2023 First Round
Finalist for the Women's Fiction Writers Association, *Red Thread of Fate*
is categorized as Romance and Women's Fiction. The criminal element
comes in, however, when the car accident that kills Tony and Mia is
dubious with Mia's angry ex as a suspect. Thus, the central plot is Tam
uncovering the mystery of Tony and Tam's relationship in China which
includes a peak into Chinese orphanages and the process of international
adoption. The story is inspired by Butler and her husband's own journey
adopting their son from China. Through this process, she expanded upon
her earlier, limited definition of family:

> Before we adopted our son, I'm embarrassed to admit that I thought "fam-
> ily" only meant those that are related to you by blood. But I realized this
> isn't true. Some people have blood relatives that they never speak to, yet call
> people they've found in life "family" because those are the people who have
> stood by them and are there for them when needed. It made me realize that
> "family" is the people you find that you want to support you through life.
> This was what I hoped to convey with *Red Thread of Fate*. That family can
> be blood-related, or it can be a found family or anything in between. ("A
> Conversation")

What is unique about *Red Thread* is that it exposes and normalizes Asian
American experiences with infertility and adoption. Contrary to popular belief,
Asian Americans do struggle with infertility and turn to adoption to complete
their family formation. What stories like this and the above demonstrate is that
flipping the script humanizes the stories behind adoption for each member of the
adoption triad. Through Kamal, we better understand the birthmother's backstory to see why relinquishment can be both a necessary choice and a forced
coercion. Through Lee, we witness how transracial adoptees struggle for
acceptance, recognition, and belonging. Finally, for adoptive parents of color,

authors like Mosley, Cosby, and Butler show how adoption is more than growing our families but reconciling with and surviving through our own struggles of not belonging in a world that never fully sees us.

3 On DNA, Searching, and Belonging

What Does DNA Do?

At fifty-four years of age, a woman takes a DNA test for fun and discovers that her devout Orthodox Jewish stockbroker father is *not* her biological father. Thus begins her investigation into family secrets of infertility and sperm donation, a meeting with her biological father, and what it means to know one's genetic history while grappling with secrets maintained between parent and child (Shapiro).

A brother and sister find each other through a 23andMe match. Unable to care for two children, their mother had given her son up for adoption days after birth. The daughter had no idea she had a brother until they were in their fifties (Hill).

Through DNA testing, an adopted woman discovers her biological father is on the FBI's Most Wanted list for murdering his mother, his wife, and their three sons. He has yet to be found (Johnson, "A Search").

The stories above illustrate the complex range of possibilities of what the journalist and author of *The Lost Family: How DNA Testing Is Upending Who We Are* Libby Copeland describes as the "consumer genomics age" (21) of recreational DNA testing. Through companies such as Ancestry.com and 23andMe, amateur genealogy detectives or "seekers" are able to uncover the mystery of their ancestry, with oftentimes surprising and life-changing results. With just a small amount of spit, anyone can disclose everything from their racial/ethnic composition to their health predisposition to finding unknown relatives. For seekers like Dani Shapiro, Jolie Pearl and Neil Schwartzman, and Kathy Gillcrist above, DNA testing also unveiled secrets intentionally concealed by their trusted family members. As a result, these seekers, usually adoptees, take on unanticipated detective roles in order to unravel the mystery of their own origins. The search is not an easy one, however. Seekers struggle through the emotional turmoil of deception while also navigating access to information hindered by legalized protections of birthparents. Oftentimes, adoption documentation is not available or incomplete. Throughout, the ethics of disclosure – does a birthparent have a right to privacy? does the adoptee have a right to their origin story? – haunt the journey. Today, for instance, only fourteen states[10] give unrestricted access to adult adoptees to their original birth certificate. The controversy over birthmothers' right to privacy is an ongoing

---

[10] These states include Alabama, Alaska, Colorado, Connecticut, Kansas, Louisiana, Maine, Massachusetts, New Hampshire, New York, Oregon, Rhode Island, South Dakota, and Vermont.

debate as evidenced by the recent Louisiana House Bill 450 (now Act 470) which allowed open access to birth certificates in 2022. Anti-abortion advocates strongly oppose unrestricted access, arguing that confidentiality is essential in making adoption an alternative to abortion (Muller). But, today, the availability and popularization of recreational DNA testing make expectations of complete privacy impossible. As the seekers examined here will show, in addition to the more than 35 million participants who submitted their genetic information to ancestry databases thus far, diligent detective work will eventually expose strangers who will find themselves connected by blood.[11]

But what does DNA information actually do? and don't do. The basis of both adoption search narratives and mystery stories is knowledge: who has access to knowledge, what secrets the knowledge unveils, and what to do with the knowledge. For Shapiro, discovering her false paternity resulted in a shocking and life-changing awareness. "I woke up one morning and life was as I had always known it to be ... By the time I went to bed that night, my entire history – the life I had lived – had crumbled beneath me, like the buried ruins of an ancient forgotten city" (13). Her devastating discovery plummeted her into an existential crisis. "Who was I? *What* was I? I felt as if I might disintegrate" (61). Shortly after her shock, DNA helps Shapiro uncover her biological father's identity. "I was on the hunt. A fact-finding mission had taken me over, keeping the deeper reservoir of feelings at bay" (42). Surprisingly, with the help of her husband and a journalist, the "trio of detectives" (56) quickly found her father through social media and YouTube, merely days after receiving her DNA results.

But the real revelation in *Inheritance* (2019) is not necessarily *who* her father is but, rather, Shapiro's slow realization of her parents' grief and their self-imposed silence behind the secrecy that haunted them throughout their lives. DNA as a detective tool may tell of one's ancestry and blood relations and may even justify one's tendencies or habits ("it's in our blood to be good at math" or "her love for spicy food is in her DNA"). But, DNA cannot tell us about who we really are, who and why we love, why we make certain choices, why we have certain likes and dislikes, and why people act a certain way. It cannot tell us why certain acts/crimes were committed (the story behind the evidence) nor why certain truths were hidden. DNA doesn't tell how secrets can plague you,

---

[11] It is important to point out that, of course, not all adoptees experience their adoption in the same way, including the desire to solve the mystery of their origins. In "23 and Not Me: As an Adoptee, I'm Not Even Remotely Tempted to Take a DNA Test," adoptee Sarah C, Baldwin writes that she never longed for the common adoptee need to know but rather "always cherished being a question mark, a cipher, a butterfly who can't be pinned" (Baldwin). Further, Baldwin writes that "there can be bliss in ignorance" and that unknowing and its subsequent ability to create multiple origin stories is, actually, where her power lies (Baldwin).

lurking around every corner. For Shapiro, the discovery gave her insight into better understanding her father's "depression, his physical and psychic pain, his decline" (226) as well as her mother's self-maintained narrative of family that she "clung to as if it were the only buoy in the sea" but that also "contributed to her becoming a miserable, alien creature, a woman who radiated rage" (231). Through her journey which includes a meeting and continued connection with her birthfather, Shapiro, in the end, reaffirms who her father is.

> I may have been cut from the same cloth as Ben Walden [her birthfather], but I was and forever would be Paul Shapiro's daughter . . . If not for him, I would never have been born. I was connected to him on the level of *neshama* [Hebrew for soul], which had nothing to do with biology, and everything to do with love. (219)

For Shapiro, DNA uncovers a mystery but it does not negate the love and connection that exist in the absence of biology.

What *need* does the adoption search meet and for whom? As Margaret Homans writes, adoptees are "peculiarly burdened, in popular adoption culture, with this obligation to find, know, and grasp material origins" (*Imprint* 114). Citing Kimberly Leighton, Homans writes that adoptees are "told they suffer from 'genealogical bewilderment' and must want to know who their 'real parents' are," displaying the "bias against 'the social acceptance of adoption as a mode of family-making as good as biological reproduction'" (*Imprint* 113–114). In addition to this burden, Homans reminds us that the adoptee search for truth via a quest for the origin story is ultimately unattainable. "Yet even the most stringently honest memoirs cannot fail to resort not only to fictional techniques in telling their stories but also to fiction in constructing the very origin whose truth is so painstakingly sought" (*Imprint* 122). Even when the adoption search is successful, additional questions arise, many of which can never be completely answered nor resolved. We only need to examine memoirs such Lisa Wool-Rim Sjöblom's *Palimpsest: Documents From a Korean Adoption* (2019), Nicole Chung's *All You Can Ever Know* (2018), and Jenny Heijun Wills's *Older Sister, Not Necessarily Related* (2019) to see that reunion does not result in catharsis or relief but rather forces confrontation with ongoing trauma and too often leaves questions unanswered and lives fragmented. As transracial adoptee Jenny Heijun Wills argues, "truth is not necessarily the end goal" (83) in adoption narratives because "adoption is not a terminal event" but rather an "ongoing circumstance" without a "satisfactory resolution" (85). Shannon Gibney, also a transracial adoptee, shows how knowing is incomplete and truth is unachievable in *The Girl I Am, Was, and Never Will Be: A Speculative Memoir of Transracial Adoption* (2023). "The only way for people like me – adoptees – to express the truth of our lives and experiences is to embrace that there are no singular truths. There is no one reality. There are no stories without holes. There are only spaces to be breathed into. Sometimes, rewritten. Always, the spaces are revered. And feared" (11). Gibney's speculative memoir plays with the idea of knowing by depicting a parallel telling of two girls, adopted Shannon and non-adopted Erin, living two different lives across an intersecting timeline to show that for adoptees, the speculative is "our 'real lives'" (12).

The Business of DNA

Although the relationship to truth may be fraught for adoptees, the promise that "DNA doesn't lie" is a strong appeal for both adoptees and non-adoptees. DNA is about knowing and knowing has become a multi-billion-dollar business. Perhaps no other cultural phenomenon has been more influential in popularizing DNA ancestry searches than shows like PBS's *African American Lives* (2006), *African American Lives 2* (2008), and *Finding Your Roots* (premiered 2012), all hosted by acclaimed historian Henry Louis Gates, Jr. These documentary series use genealogical research (written documents) and genetic analysis (DNA testing) to uncover family histories of dozens of celebrities and non-celebrities alike. For instance, former House Speaker Paul Ryan, who identifies as Irish Catholic, learned that he is 3 percent Ashkenazi Jew (*FYR*, Season 5, Episode 6). Controversy halted Season 3 of *Finding Your Roots* when actor Ben Affleck discovered he had a slave-owning ancestor and tried to censor that information from the public. Of course, stories about adoption and the revelation of paternity/maternity have been some of the more moving stories to emerge, including radio host, civil rights activist, and Gates's close friend, Joe Madison, who learned that his father is not his biological father (Season 5, Episode 10), or comedian Adam Samberg, who found his adopted mother's birthmother (Season 5, Episode 1), or singer L. L. Cool J. and his mother simultaneously discovering her own adoption secret (Season 3, Episode 7).

Today, adoption agencies like Adoptions With Love (adoptionswithlove.org) advertise and support open adoptions so that these types of family secrets are no longer the norm. According to the Adoptions With Love website, 95 percent of adoption agencies today offer open adoption and 99 percent of adoptees know of their adoption by age five. Interestingly, they also recommend *not* taking a DNA test:

> Sure, anyone looking for information regarding their biological roots can purchase a DNA kit, made popular by companies like "23 and Me" and

Ancestry.com. However, for those who have been touched by adoption, this is not always recommended. Those in closed adoptions should work with their adoption agency to conduct a proper search, or to reach out to their birth parents with the help of an adoption social worker. Adoptions With Love has an active search and reunion program for those looking for more information about their biological families. (Rosenhaus)

Of course, it is the business of adoption agencies to attract potential birthmothers so that for any who are uneasy about adopting their child out, open adoptions seem an attractive solution. Agencies also recognize, however, that not all birthmothers want to maintain contact and that some adoptions occur due to tragedies beyond the normal reasons such as teenage pregnancy or economic instability. As such, cautions like the above serve as subtle warnings for seekers with agencies serving as buffers between triad members.

But, today, searching for their biological family is still certainly a common goal among adoptees, especially since many adoptions, particularly international ones, rarely have the openness adoption agencies like the above tout. Experts include investigative genetics genealogist CeCe Moore, whose biography describes her as "an innovator and pioneer in the use of autosomal DNA to resolve unknown parentage and family mysteries [and is] frequently consulted by DNA testing companies, genealogists, adoptees, law enforcement and the press" (CeCeMoore.com). Her ABC documentary series, *The Genetic Detective* (ABC), shows Moore working closely with law enforcement to identify victims and perpetrators. As her website boasts, Moore has identified over 200 violent criminals and her work "has led to the first conviction, the first conviction through jury verdict, and the first exoneration in criminal cases" (CeCeMoore.com). Moore also works as a consultant for Gates's *Finding Your Roots* series, demonstrating the intertwining, parallel narratives of DNA, adoption, and crime.

In addition to the cultural popularity of shows like the above, DNA has become a massive business in recent years. At least 246 genetics testing companies across the globe are selling their services with light regulation (Copeland 54). In 2019, it was estimated that more than 26 million consumers added their DNA to databases with a projection rate of 100 million by 2021 (Regalado). According to DataHorizon Research, the genetic testing market is valued at USD 7.8 billion in 2022 and is expected to reach USD 19 billion by 2032 ("Genetic"). While some benefits have been revealed with DNA testing, such as the capture of the Golden State Killer in 2018, other possibilities demonstrate how DNA can also be used to weaponize and harm. In October 2023, 23andMe, one of the world's leading DNA testing companies, confirmed that their data was hacked. The hackers posted a sample and put up for sale a list of people with Ashkenazi Jewish ancestry and Chinese ancestry (Newman). Today, DNA has become both crystal ball and weapon utilized to maintain genetic discrimination.

Searching

In many ways, adoption search narratives mirror a detective story. The seeker, usually the adoptee, is confronted by a mystery – the relinquishment and adoption – and gathers clues in order to find the birthparents to solve that mystery. As a story of detection, the adoption search narrative oftentimes fails because many adoptees, especially international adoptees, run into an informational wall when gathering evidence. *Found* (2021), for instance, is a documentary film that focuses on three adopted teenage girls who discover they are blood-related cousins through 23andMe. After meeting, they travel to China and work with a genealogist to find answers about their family histories. The genealogist also works with the Chinese birthfamilies who are hoping to reunite with the babies they relinquished but never stopped loving. In a moving moment at the film's end, we witness one adoptee, Lily, whose DNA does not match a potential family. The non-match is devastating for both Lily and the birthfamily. But, as disappointing as this moment is for her, witnessing the birthfamily's devastation helps confirm for her that birthparents love and desperately seek the children they were forced to give up. "I've just gotten a deeper understanding of my birthparents. I can just see from their point of view. No parent would just, like, willingly give up their baby. And, like, I would just say that [the failed search] kinda helped" (*Found*). While the search is unsuccessful, Lily's awareness of birthparents' love brings a sense of peace and understanding she didn't know she needed.

Reading the adoption narrative as intricately connected to the mystery/crime story is evidenced in A. M. Homes's *The Mistress's Daughter* (2007), a memoir about adoptee Homes being reunited with her birthparents thirty years after relinquishment. *The Mistress's Daughter*, however, is an unusual search narrative in that it reverses the search trope by *beginning* with reunion and ending with the search. Homes's memoir illustrates how a reunion can potentially backfire when a member of the adoption triad (in this case, the adoptee) is not prepared for reunification. The first half of the memoir, Book One, begins with Homes's birthmother contacting her for a reunion. The scene of relinquishment as described to Homes comes directly out of a noir film:

> I met my parents for the first time in a car parked around the corner from the hospital. They sat parked on a street in downtown Washington in the middle of a snowstorm, waiting for me to be delivered to them. They brought

clothing to dress me, to disguise me, to begin to make me their own. This undercover pickup and delivery was made by a friend who purposely dressed in ratty old clothes – her costume designed not to attract attention, not to give information ... My parents sat in the car, worrying, while the neighbor went into the hospital to collect me. This was a secret mission, something could go wrong. *She* – the mother – could change her mind. They sat waiting, and then the neighbor was there walking through the snow with a bundle in her arms. She handed me to my mother, and my parents brought me home, mission accomplished ... There is something inescapably sordid about the way the story unfolds. I was adopted, purchased, ordered, and picked up like a cake from a bakery. (14–15)

Later, the neighbor friend admits that the secrecy was demanded from both sides. "I wore bad clothing ... I disguised myself. I didn't want her to know anything. And she too was very concerned about anyone knowing who she was ... 'If you ever see me, don't acknowledge me,' the woman said" (16–17). As Homes describes, "[t]he amount of mystery that surrounded the proceedings was enormous, everything was subtext and secrecy" (16). Thirty years after this secretive transfer, Homes is no less mystified by her birthparents' behavior. They are both eccentric, demanding, and inappropriate. Her birthmother gets upset at Homes when she doesn't send her a Valentine's card and tells Homes *she* should adopt *her*. The birthfather only wants to meet in hotel bars and lobbies, admitting when they first meet that he is not circumcised. Through these encounters, Homes realizes that their reunion is more about their needs than her own. "The fact is that whatever each of them is in this for has nothing to do with me – it is not about my need, my desire, and for the moment I have had enough" (93). As she states, "adoptees don't really have rights, their lives are about supporting the secrets, the needs and desires of others" (20). Further, within this rightless status, Homes acknowledges that adoptees can never escape their role to fit in, to assimilate. "To be adopted is to be adapted, to be amputated and sewn back together again. Whether or not you regain full function, there will always be scar tissue" (54).

It is not until the second half of the memoir, Book Two, seven years after her birthmother passes, that Homes begins to ponder her birthmother's life and identity. In perusing boxes labeled *Dead Ellen 1–4*, a mixture of random items Homes gathered soon after her birthmother's death and stored – "She put me up for adoption – I'm sending her to ministorage" (117) – Homes begins to construct her birthmother's life. It is one filled with contradictions of high society photos mixed with dozens of unopened bills, threatening letters from banks and lawyers, real estate transactions gone wrong, and pharmacy receipts piled atop thank-you letters for donations and gifts. Surrounded by the mountains of paper clues, Homes imagines how her birthparents' lives may have been prior to her birth. She becomes a self-proclaimed "twenty-first century Sherlock Holmes" (146) via genealogical websites such as Ancestry.com and JewishGen as well as numerous archives. She unearths information on several past generations and communicates with people across the country and internationally to recreate her family story. She hires researchers and graduate students to help her months-long search. Her search stops, however, when Homes confronts her birthfather, who refuses to share the results of a DNA test they took years earlier to confirm his paternity. Lawyers become involved but struggle to determine Homes's legal rights of accessing her own DNA results. In a chapter titled "Like an Episode of *L.A. Law*," Homes imagines her birthfather being deposed in court. Finally, with her father's silence and ultimate rejection, Homes recalls her adoptive maternal grandmother, her inspiration to become a writer and teller of stories, and realizes that she is a product of "all four threads [of her family narratives] that twist and rub against one another, the fusion and friction combining to make me who and what I am . . . I am also influenced by another narrative; the story of what it is to be the adopted one, the chosen one, the outsider brought in" (234). Rather than understanding adoption as a cutting off and loss of family, Homes accepts it as an extension of family. As Homes concludes her memoir, "Did I choose to be found? No. Do I regret it? No. I couldn't not know" (238).

Belonging

The meaning of what it means *to know* is especially complex in the adoption crime narrative, intermingling the detection of crime with the discovery of identity. Scott Lasser's *The Year That Follows* (2009) is a multiple adoption story about knowing, secrets, and kinship. When Cat's brother, Kyle, dies during the 9/11 attacks, the crime that serves as the background to the story, she grapples with his death alongside his recent confession that he has an infant son from a brief affair. Determined to find her brother's last blood legacy, the baby who symbolizes "continuity" (239) of the family name, Cat searches for him into the following year of Kyle's death. She discovers that the birthmother also perished in the attacks and that the baby is being raised by her grandparents. When Cat visits them, she learns that the grandfather has terminal cancer and they allow her to adopt him. Significantly, they refuse a DNA test to confirm paternity because they, knowing their daughter, don't see a need. Alongside Cat's search is a parallel story of her and Kyle's father, Sam, who has his own secret he wants to confess to Cat: she is not his biological daughter. Unbeknownst to Sam, however, Cat has known about her paternity from her recently deceased mother and was waiting for her father to acknowledge it. Throughout the story, anxiety about bloodlines, adopted versus biological kinship love, and family secrets and silences create isolation between father and daughter. When Cat tells Sam about Kyle's son, he is "moved ... [because t]he boy is in his blood; some part of Kyle is still alive" (183), leaving Cat to be further distanced from his concept of family. *The Year That Follows* is, in essence, a story about family secrets and the silences they keep. This is emphasized in the climactic conclusion when Cat's scientist lover admits he secretly took a DNA test of the baby and announces that the baby is not Kyle's biological son after all. Cat's motivation in mothering the baby becomes clear at this revelation:

> I'm supposed to be raising Kyle's son. *Kyle's*. It's how she thinks of Ian [the baby], as Kyle's. Ian is about love and family and continuity, a Miller – that's his name now, Ian Miller – a part of a small and unlikely family. She is supposed to be carrying on the family, extending it. Ian is hers, and yet he is the child of strangers. (239, emphasis in original)

Although Cat keeps the baby in the end, the story concludes with Cat and her lover trying for a biological baby of their own, "[o]ne who's wholly yours and mine" (219). In this story, family may be formed by adoption, but blood bonds signify true connection and belonging.

Unlike *The Year That Follows*, how much DNA matters in determining a sense of belonging or in predetermining one's identity is often examined through the nature-versus-nurture debate. International bestselling author and former physician, award-winning Tess Gerritsen is known for her romantic thrillers, her medical thrillers, and, in particular, the Rizzoli & Isles series. Gerritsen's *Body Double* (2004) is the fourth in the Rizzoli & Isles series that features Boston homicide detective Jane Rizzoli and medical examiner Dr. Maura Isles. In *Body Double*, Dr. Isles returns home from a medical conference to discover that an unknown twin sister, Anna Leoni, is murdered just outside her home. As Rizzoli and Isles begin their investigation and through DNA testing, they uncover Isles's past of a murderous, psychotic birthfamily who kidnapped pregnant women and sold their babies. Isles learns that her birthparents, Amalthea and her cousin Elijah, sold their own twin baby girls – Maura and Anna – which began their series of national, decades-long kidnappings and murders. Upon her discovery, Dr. Isles struggles with the nature-versus-nurture question. As an adoptee who was unaware of her twin sister, she repeatedly questions the relevance of DNA to identity and the eerily similar individual choices each twin made. For instance, both Maura and Anna are/were scientists and, therefore, "governed by intellect ... take comfort in facts" (97), both had the same identical products in their medicine cabinets ("Right down to our choice of flu medicines, she thought, we were identical" [132]), and both even had similar bedroom décor ("*Like my bedroom*, thought Maura" [132, emphasis in original]). But whatever the similarities, the message of the novel is clear on adoptee searches: "Adoptees are often curious about their origins. For some of them it becomes an obsession. So they go on document hunts. Invest thousands of dollars and a lot of heartache searching for mothers who don't want to be found. And if they *do* find them, it's seldom the fairy-tale ending they expected. That's what [Anna] was looking for, Detective. A fairy-tale ending. Sometimes they're better off just forgetting it, and moving on with their lives" (159–160). When Maura finally uncovers the mystery of her parentage and wrestles with her genetic connection to murderers, she proclaims to her birth-mother that "[b]lood means nothing … no matter what the DNA may say, you're not my mother" (390). Further, "[i]n her veins flowed the blood of murderers. But evil was not hereditary. Though she might carry its potential in her genes, so too did every child ever born. *In this, I am no different. We are all descended from monsters*" (390–391, emphasis in original).

The nature-versus-nurture question also becomes the underlying question in Edgar Award-nominated and Agatha, Anthony, and Mary Higgins-Clark Award-winning author Lori Rader-Day's *The Death of Us* (2023) via the role of biological versus adopted motherhood. Liss and Link Kehoe are recently married when Liss discovers her husband is a serial cheater. One rainy night, Link's mistress, Ashley Hays, hands over her and Link's infant son, Callan, to Liss and disappears. Hays is never seen again and Liss becomes a stepmother to Callan. As a stepparent to her husband's illegitimate son, Liss struggles with validating her maternal role and identity, unable to officially adopt Callan due to Ashley's suspended, unknown status.

> And didn't it sting a little? She had put her whole heart into being Callan's mother, far more effort than Link had put into being his dad. Link could do no wrong, even as he *did*. Link simply *was* a parent. She had been forced to turn herself into one to swallow her self-doubt that she was the right kind. To ignore that she was his mother *and* she wasn't, both at the same time. (155, emphasis in original)

We witness Liss's insecurity about her mother role throughout when she is required to get annual written permission from Link to make medical decisions for Callan, for instance, or when a friend reminds her that Callan is not really hers. Liss's role as mother, however, is quickly solidified when Ashley's remains are discovered in the pond on the Kehoe property. DNA tests reveal that the body is not only long-lost Ashley's but that Link is not Callan's father but rather his *brother*. It turns out that Key Kehoe, Link's father and former police chief, was also a serial cheater who had an affair with Ashley. What is ultimately revealed is that Key's wife, Patty, killed Ashley in order to protect her family. In the end, Liss also protects her family by keeping the genetic relationship between her now-ex Link and son Callan a secret. Here, DNA facts would devastate this family and, as a result, family secrets are maintained. *The Death of Us* is in many ways a story about women protecting their family from the damage created by their husbands. It is the mothers in the story – Liss, Patty, Ashley – who safeguard their sons from disturbing knowledge, showing that although DNA may reveal family secrets, it does not always have to be confined by them.

Rejecting DNA as the ultimate indicator of belonging is the outcome of forensic psychologist/mystery writer Ellery Kane's *The Wrong Family* (2023). When Hallie Sherman receives notice from Family Ties DNA letting her know that they found a "first degree paternal match" (3), she wants to believe she'll finally belong to a family. Her drug-addicted mother died from a tragic car accident when she was nine, leaving her in foster home after foster home. Reuniting with her father, Robert Thompson, and his family at their idyllic home in Lake Tahoe seems unreal until strange occurrences begin to disrupt their lives climaxing with murder. *The Wrong Family* is a novel about a DNA-inspired reunion that quickly turns into a mystery of family secrets, sibling rivalry, arson, and murder. Although the DNA match between Hallie and Robert is ultimately revealed to be falsified, the revelation that the murderer and arsonist is Robert's troubled son at the end of the novel emphasizes that sharing DNA does not necessarily result in familial harmony nor kinship. When Hallie receives another potential DNA match in the Epilogue, she realizes that "what I've been searching for isn't a person, it's a feeling. A feeling of belonging. I have to find that for myself" (393). Belonging, it turns out, is not necessarily achieved through DNA.

In addition to uniting unknown family members, DNA can help solve crimes. When Liz Catalino's cousin, Andie, gifts her a 23andMe kit for her birthday, she is shocked to discover that she was adopted at birth. Furthermore, Liz is even more surprised to learn that her birthmother gave birth in prison while incarcerated for drug charges. Thus begins Steph Mullin & Nicole Mabry's *The Family Tree* (2021). Although her adoptive parents kept this from Liz in order to protect her, she feels an urgent need to find her unknown relatives. "I was hurt at being left in the dark about my own life by so many people, intentional or not. The only thing that would make me feel better, I decided, was to know everything. To take back control" (155). For Liz, searching is about taking back control of a life she realized she never had. When she gives permission for law enforcement to access her DNA, Liz learns she is genetically related to the Tri-State Killer, a serial killer who has been abducting and killing pairs of women for forty years. When Liz meets her biological uncle, Cris, she must navigate uniting with a family member while also playing amateur detective alongside the FBI. Liz suspects Cris may be the killer, but eventually helps uncover the killer as Cris's cousin, Frank, who had an obsessive need to control women. In the end, Liz is reunited with her biological father and half-brother through DNA testing. The story concludes with Liz reading a *NYTimes* article about a bill being reviewed by the New York legislature to allow adoptees unrestricted access to their original birth certificates.

In adoptions where the adoption is obvious on the surface, namely transracial adoptions, what it means *to know* has layered complications. With transracial adoptions, outsiders can easily recognize the adoptee, oftentimes creating an outsider positionality and awareness for the adoptee. Clearly detectable, transracial adoptees cannot easily blend in with their families. For the transracial adoptees, especially those raised in predominantly White locations, this immediate knowing forces them to struggle through their adopted identity *and* their racial identity (see Carroll, Gibney, Trenka, Wills, Chung). Of course, the relationship between DNA and scientific racism, our inability to come to terms with our history of slavery and imperialism, and the continued disenfranchisement of BIPOC communities will always remind us of our fractured and fraught understandings of who belongs. The adoption crime stories below reflect some of the anxieties behind this troubled history.

John Straley's *So Far and Good* (2021) shows how DNA testing exposes family secrets that would otherwise have been kept hidden. When Georgianna (aka George) swabs her sleeping mom's cheek for a birthday DNA surprise, it is George who is shocked to discover that she is not biologically related to her mother, Ida Paul, at all. Soon after discovery, Ida admits that she kidnapped George as a newborn while also faking her own pregnancy. George is actually the infamous "Baby Jane Doe" whose kidnapping was publicized internationally. To make matters worse, Ida is a White Democratic legislator who kidnapped the baby from a Native Tlingit woman. But, when Ida commits suicide in jail and her husband, Mr. Paul, is imprisoned for aiding Ida, George meets her biological parents, Kristy and Thomas Thompson, with her custody in question. Reuniting with her biological parents unearths more family secrets filled with locked basements, aberrant sexuality coupled with violent behavior, prison escapes, and murder. It is revealed that Thomas Thompson has a history of bondage and violence, seriously beating girls in his basement. By the end, Thomas is jailed and Kristy admits that she and Ida planned the fake kidnapping in order to get baby George away from Thomas. Mr. Paul, also Tlingit, had wanted a half-Tlingit, half-White baby and went along with the plan. With Thomas jailed, Mr. Paul is freed for saving baby George from danger. In an interesting turn of events, George is left with her biological mother and nonbiological father, both Tlingit, in a literary move that keeps Natives with Natives. *So Far and Good* is the rare adoption story where the adoptee remains with her birthmother and has even greater access to her birth heritage.

If *So Far So Good* gives a nod to Indian Child Welfare Act (ICWA) in returning George to her racial heritage, Ellen Crosby's *The Harvest of Secrets* (2018) shows how DNA can reveal racial skeletons in the not-so-White family trees. *The Harvest of Secrets* is the ninth novel in the Wine Country Mysteries Series which centers on Lucie Montgomery, the owner of the Montgomery Estate Vineyard in Atoka, Virginia. It is busy harvest season when a skull is discovered buried near the estate cemetery. Shortly after this discovery, the handsome aristocrat and owner of a neighboring vineyard, Jean-Claude de Merignac, is found murdered. As Lucie tries to solve the double mystery, she is shocked to discover that in response to a recent DNA ancestry test she took, she learns her father had an illegitimate son, her half-brother, from a brief affair years ago. This revelation and the subsequent parallel stories of the skull mystery and her half-brother become the novel's focus. De Merignac's murderer is ultimately detected to be a scorned lover but lays out the novel's larger commentary on forbidden love. When Lucie connects with her half-brother, David, she is surprised to discover he is mixed-race with an African American birthmother. This discovery corresponds with her uncovering of the skull's mystery, revealed to be a relative from the mid-nineteenth century who was murdered due to her love for a Black man. David explains to Lucie about interracial marriage being a crime until *Loving v. Virginia* in 1967. "'Illegal' as in being sentenced to a year in jail because they fell in love with someone they were told they couldn't love. That it was a damned crime" (240). Discovering the skull's history and meeting her biracial half-brother launch Lucie's racial awakening. Throughout her search journey, Lucie learns the perils of knowledge and realizes that not everyone wants to know.

> David's birthmother did not want to acknowledge him and as difficult and heartbreaking as that was for him to accept, she was within her rights to do so. As I realized when I opened Pandora's box and explored my DNA and my family history, I couldn't stuff what spilled out back inside. Sometimes – like now – you just had to live with *knowing* and that's it. (308 emphasis in original)

Both discoveries reveal the secrets created due to societal taboos, past and present, against interracial love. Although DNA may give you the factual knowledge of genetic relations, it cannot answer all the questions hidden behind that fact. Lucie realizes that "[*t*]*he blood of your parents is not lost in you*. But it didn't have to define you" (308).

Wendy Corsi Staub's The Foundlings Trilogy incorporates DNA, serial killers, U.S. history of anti-Black racism, and an adoptee search journey. When Amelia Crenshaw's mother lies dying in the hospital, she discovers that she is not her biological daughter. Abandoned at a Harlem church, Amelia is discovered and adopted by the church janitor and his wife, Calvin and Bettina Crenshaw. Thus begins Amelia's search for her identity in Wendy Corsi Staub's *Little Girl Lost* (2019), the first in the Foundlings Trilogy. In this introduction, Amelia's discovery of her parentage coincides with her adopted mother's death. Thus, she spends most of the book angry and lost. When Amelia sees a Barbara Walters interview with adoptee Dr. Silas Moss, a professor of genetics and molecular biology at Cornell, and his research using DNA to reunite birth-families with their children, she travels to Ithaca to seek Dr. Moss's help. Interwoven with Amelia's search is a parallel plot of a psychotic serial killer who raped teenaged girls twenty years prior and murdered their families. All four girls became pregnant, with one keeping the baby, one self-aborting, and two relinquishing their babies. As Amelia is trying to uncover her own abandoned past, the killer and his followers return to kill the four surviving teen girls, now women, and their children. The second novel in the series, *Dead Silence* (2019), takes place twenty-nine years after *Little Girl Lost*. Now, Amelia is an investigative genealogist and a consultant to *The Roots and Branches Project*, a program similar to PBS's *Finding Your Roots* and *African American Lives*. While this novel's plot focuses on a little boy foundling, the question of ethics around DNA testing becomes central in *Dead Silence*. While Amelia struggles with the ethical dilemma of testing the boy's DNA, she discovers that through her own DNA results she is, in fact, genetically related to her adopted mother. The third novel of the series, *The Butcher's Daughter* (2020), uncovers the mystery of Amelia's birth that includes forbidden love between her White mother and Black father, the KKK, and a kidnapping. Amelia's birthfather's mother arranges to kidnap newly born Amelia in order to safeguard her and her birthmother from the KKK. In the end, Amelia reunites with her birthmother and declares, "I'm home" (458).

In Elle Marr's *Strangers We Know* (2022), what to do with the knowledge gained is the central question in this adoptee search narrative. When Ivy Hon takes a DNA test to help identify her mystery illness, she is shocked to discover that she is genetically related to the Full Moon Killer, a serial killer targeting young women in the Pacific Northwest. Through the DNAcorn website, Ivy is easily able to identify a maternal first cousin, Lottie, which begins her introduction to other biological family members. Knowing her connection to a killer, Ivy ponders about the nature-versus-nurture question:

> Blood doesn't lie, or so the saying goes. I just wish I knew whether that applies to adopted blood. Does adopted blood most closely identify with those who gave it life? Or does the family who raised the adopted blood have the most influence? Nature or nurture – I'd love to know what's responsible for the splitting headache burrowing into my skull. (1)

Although the headache may allude to her genetic disposition to lupus later on in the story, it also functions metaphorically to highlight the emotional and psychological contradictions of what it means to belong as an adoptee. Ivy recognizes that she was "loved deeply" (5) by her adopted parents and that "though [she] sometimes felt at odds with [her] laser-focused parents and brother, [she] never contacted [her] birth family. Nor they [her]" (5). Further, she admits that she was "always grateful that [her] birth mother gave [her] up so that [she] could be placed with a family that wanted [her], that guided [her], that argued with [her] when [she] was wrong and forgave [her] when [she] asked" (13). But, although the decision to search for her birth family may have been medically driven, Ivy also can never escape her adoptee identity, especially since she is a transracial adoptee. A common trope for adoptees is the sense of being othered marked by their physical difference, especially for transracial adoptees raised by White parents. For biracial Ivy (she is half-White, half-Chinese), her physical features would always distinguish her from her adopted family.

> Growing up, people complimented me in grocery stores as I stood next to my mother; they'd say that I had her beautiful bone structure – high cheekbones, small chin, wide temples. Mom would always accept the well-intentioned comment, but I would blush knowing I couldn't possibly share her features genetically. (124)

So, when Ivy meets her biological family and they comment on her physical similarity to her birthmother – "Your forehead, I think. Or your nose. I don't know, it just feels like I'm talking to some alternate universe version of my sister again" (125) – or when she perceives similar habits from her biological maternal grandmother – "Aggie twists her lips to the side, a quirk I have when I'm thinking" (159) – she feels a "warmth" (158) inside her, an emotional pang that tells her she belongs to this family.

For Ivy, while DNA shows biological connection to her birth family, it also opens up mysteries of her origin story that is hurtful to hear. When her biological uncle (who turns out to be a killer in the end) tells Ivy she was the product of a "transactional acquaintance" (170), Ivy consciously reaffirms

her parents' love for her (nurture) and rejects any notion of hereditary impli-
cations (nature):

> I try to remember who I am – my parents' daughter. Harold and Vivian Hon
> adopted me within days of my birth, deliberately and intentionally, as they
> had desired a little girl to round out their family for years. Lots of adopted
> babies are surprises to those who conceived them. All of them are ultimately
> wanted by the parents who choose to raise and love them. Even though this
> news hits me like a punch to the throat, I'm no different. (171)

As Ivy continues her double quest to uncover her birthparents as well as to help
solve the Full Moon Killer's identity, the real search is for Ivy to come to terms
with her adoption. By the end of *Strangers We Know*, the killers are identified
(her biological grandmother and uncle) and Ivy is reunited with both her birthparents (her birthmother escaped her family's cult and eventually reunited with
the birthfather). As Ivy concludes,

> Now, as I steal glances at my birth parents, I wonder whether I just needed
> someone to say it's not my fault I was given up, even if it's irrational. That
> everyone genuinely did the best they could with the time they had with me.
> That no one wanted to leave, either my birth or my adoptive parents, but
> circumstances – life – required it. (266)

Writing as a daughter of an adoptee (Acknowledgements), Elle Marr shows that
regardless of so much negative attention the practice of adoption has garnered
recently, for many, adoption is a practice of love and compassion needed in
a world that desperately needs it. More importantly, there is no single adoption
story including no single reason why seekers choose to search. As Nicole Chung
writes in her memoir:

> For all my wondering and questions as a child, it's taken me a long time to
> understand that, as adopters and adoptee, my parents and I will always view
> my adoption in vastly different ways. *There are some things your parents
> are never going to fully understand, just because they have never experi-
> enced being adopted*, a fellow adoptee told me years ago, but I decided to
> search for my birth family. The questions that sometimes kept me awake at
> night, the ones I hoarded and kept to myself, afraid to even scribble in my
> diary, did not haunt my mother and father at all. It took me many years to
> recognize and give voice to this fundamental dissonance: their gain was
> mine, too, but only after I experienced a deep loss. (209–210, emphasis in
> original)

To seek, then, is to acknowledge that there are multiple stories and multiple
reasons for seeking. It is to accept that not everyone will understand the journey
itself nor are they meant to. To rely on a single truth, whether DNA-supported or

not, is to miss the range of truths. In a mystery story where uncovering truth is the goal, this may be unnerving. For the adoption story, especially from the adoptee perspective, not knowing is part of the trauma of loss and grief.

Coda

As I was finishing *Bloodlines*, Susan Kiyo Ito's memoir *I Would Meet You Anywhere* (2023) was released. I was immediately struck by the memoir's description because it tells of a biracial adoptee (half Japanese, half White) who is adopted by nisei Japanese Americans. Adoptive parents of color are rare in both fiction and creative nonfiction. As an Asian American transracial adoptive mother, I was instantly drawn to Ito's memoir and devoured it in mere hours. *I Would Meet You Anywhere* is a beautifully written and vulnerable life story that took decades to write. Ito's reunion with her birthmother exposes the conflicting afterlife of search and reunion. Their relationship is both intimate and tense, frustrating and tragic. For decades, Ito was at her birthmother's whim, an emotional push and pull that reached its peak when Ito would inquire about her birthfather's identity. Her birthmother would get angry at her questioning and kept his identity hidden from her. Ito eventually found her birthfather when she took a DNA test. Unfortunately, he died shortly before her discovery and was unable to meet him.

Ito's memoir tells of an adoptee's journey to her origin story and the tenuous relationship of an adoptee to her birthmother. But, much more than that, Ito's memoir reveals the adoptee's struggle with the burden of secrecy. "Since the start of my life, I have been a secret, my existence a wild inconvenience . . . For decades, I held my birthmother's secret" (240). From Ito being her birthmother's secret to the government's hold of Ito's birth records as a secret, secrecy is the hidden crime that Ito has to fight again and again. In a chapter titled "A Small Crime," Ito writes about masquerading as a pregnant woman in order to steal her own hospital records from a doctor's office. Later, she reveals how she finally received her records when then New York governor Andrew Cuomo opened access to adult adoptees in 2019. In many ways, although adoption is often criminalized in popular consciousness as we have seen in Section 1, the unsaid crime is that, even today, many adoptees are denied access to basic information about their identities. This, in essence, is criminal.

Ito's memoir and the many stories, both fiction and creative nonfiction, examined in this study have helped me better understand the complex ways adoption has affected people's lives. Although much of the works explored here reveal the dark side of humanity, these stories helped me confront some of my own anxieties of motherhood, particularly adoptive motherhood. Further, these stories have also shed light on my own lack of awareness around adoption, a void I continue to fill through reading, writing, and teaching. As my family begins our own search and reunion journey to hopefully connect with the birth family, my fears and insecurities have come to the surface and echo much of the concerns displayed here. Will I still be the "real" mother? What devastating facts will my daughter uncover? Will the birthmother want a reunion? If so, what would a dual-family situation look like? If not, how will my daughter react to rejection? Will I/we be enough for her? Will the birthmother judge the way I mothered her child? With these questions, I understand why adoptive families, especially adoptive parents, remain content to keep the information from their adopted children. As parents, we want to protect our children by any means necessary. But, also as a parent, I don't want my daughters to hide from difficulty nor be burdened with secrets. Ito's memoir exposes how secrets can haunt you, stalling and taking over your life. In the end, she comes to terms with the knowledge that no matter how hard and how long she searches, she will never get all the answers. "My time of asking questions is done," she says. "There are so many things I will never fully know or understand" (240). I know my daughter will have lots of questions, especially *after* she meets her birth family. Some will be openly vocalized; some will remain hidden in her heart. My role now, I know, is to stand by her alongside each and every one of these questions. This will be a journey, after all, for both of us. Along the way, I take with me Maya Angelou's creed that "a mother's love liberates" to show her that, even with freedom, whether or not all her questions are answered, my love will always be near.

Works Cited

"#flipthescript." Thelostdaughters.com. www.thelostdaughters.com/p/flipthe script.html. Accessed January 21, 2024.

"A Conversation with Lynn Liao Butler." Clairefy. February 1, 2022. www .clairefyblog.com/2022/02/a-conversation-with-lyn-liao-butler.html. Accessed November 17, 2023.

"Adopted Man Learns He Was Stolen from Birth Mom in Chile." *ABCNews Nightline*. April 12, 2022. www.youtube.com/watch?v=QxATWiBPXMM. Accessed August 16, 2023.

"Adoptee Deported by U.S. to Sue South Korea, Adoption Agency." *NBCNews*. January 23, 2019. www.nbcnews.com/news/asian-america/adoptee-deported-u-s-sue-south-korea-adoption-agency-n961776. Accessed August 16, 2023.

"Adoption Nightmare Prompts Suit: Family: Former San Diego Couple Tell of Falling Under Spell of 3-Year-Old Boy, Now a 16-Year-Old with a Long Record of Violence." *Los Angeles Times*. September 20, 1992. www.latimes .com/archives/la-xpm-1992-09-20-me-1638-story.html. Accessed August 16, 2023.

Alexie, Sherman. *Indian Killer*. New York: Grove Press, 1996.

Allingham, Margery. *The China Governess*. London: Ipso Books, 2016. First published in 1962.

Asgarian, Roxanna. *We Were Once a Family: A Story of Love, Death, and Child Removal in America*. New York: Farrar, Straus, and Giroux, 2023.

Baldwin, Sarah C. "23 and Not Me: As an Adoptee, I'm Not Even Remotely Tempted to Take a DNA Test." *Salon*. December 7, 2021. www.salon.com/ 2021/12/07/adopted-dna-test-genetic-ancestry-identity/. Accessed November 19, 2023.

Briggs, Laura. *How All Politics Became Reproductive Politics*. Oakland, CA: University of California Press, 2018.

"Making Abortion Illegal Does Not Lead to More Adoptions." *Adoption & Culture*, vol. 10, no. 2, 2022, pp. 251–255.

Somebody's Children: The Politics of Transracial and Transnational Adoption. Durham: Duke University Press, 2012.

Brown, Maressa. "As Black Parents Raising a White Child, We Face Racism Every Day." *Parents*. February 26, 2023. www.parents.com/parenting/ dynamics/as-black-parents-raising-a-white-child-we-face-racism-every day/#:~:text=When%20the%20Baldwins%20decided%20to,for%20fam ilies%20like%20their%20own.&text=Eight%20years%20ago%2C%20Keia%20Jones,eager%20to%20expand%20their%20family. Accessed November 15, 2023.

Butler, Lyn Liao. *Red Thread of Fate*. New York: Berkley, 2022.

Carroll, Rebecca. *Surviving the White Gaze*. New York: Simon & Schuster, 2021.

Chamberlain, Diane. *Pretending to Dance*. New York: St. Martin's Press, 2015.

Christie, Agatha. *Ordeal by Innocence*. New York: Penguin, 2011. First published 1958.

Chung, Nicole. *All You Can Ever Know*. New York: Catapult, 2018.

Copeland, Libby. *The Lost Family: How DNA Testing Is Upending Who We Are*. New York: Abrams Press, 2020.

Cosby, Shawn Andre *Razorblade Tears*. New York: Macmillan, 2021.

Crosby, Ellen. *The Harvest of Secrets*. New York: Minotaur, 2018.

"Genetic Testing Market Size to Reach USD 19.0 Billion by 2032." *DataHorizon Research*. September 12, 2023. https://finance.yahoo.com/news/genetic-testing-market-size-reach-121500628.html?guccounter=1&guce_referrer=aHR0cHM6Ly93d3cuZ29vZ2xlLmNvbS8&guce_referrer_sig=AQAAAI4vA1GvOSA7-KkIsdcCbTGroPYse0fuRrwuhTLRCVZEYtsfRlsO0VcIFj5UfO0HKECJ7DoVrbVbZMGK7NMxEhlP2ZRqw7sHgK-M_qYMEVhzRcIdYVFSQkbZgPJB7r0J07jEE4GOdwxfmD3aCa0T2pCy6a6tvg1oBH2WqGh2GOUk#:~:text=According%20to%20DataHorizzon%20Research%2C%20the, with%20a%20CAGR%20of%209.4%25. Accessed Nov. 20, 2023.

Fessler, Ann. *The Girls Who Went Away*. New York: Penguin, 2006.

Gates Jr., Henry Louis, William R. Grant, and Peter W. Kunhardt, Executive Producers. *African American Lives*. PBS. Kunhardt Productions, thirteen WNET, and Inkwell Films. 2006-2008.

Gates Jr., Henry Louis, Writer and Executive Producer. *Finding Your Roots*. PBS. Kunhardt McGee Productions, Inkwell Films, and Ark Media. March 2012-Present.

Gardner, Lisa. *The Other Daughter*. New York: Bantam, 1999.

Gerritsen, Tess. *Body Double*. New York: Ballantine, 2005. First published 2004.

Gibney, Shannon. *The Girl I Am, Was, and Never Will Be*. New York: Dutton, 2023.

Gilbert, Suzanne. *Tapioca Fire*. N.p., CreateSpace Independent Publishing, 2013.

Glaser, Gabrielle. *American Baby: A Mother, a Child, and the Secret History of Adoption*. New York: Penguin, 2021.

Goldman, Russell. "An Adoption Nightmare." *ABCNews*. May 14, 2008. https://abcnews.go.com/International/story?id=4823713&page=1. Accessed August 16, 2023.

Grinberg, Emanuella. "The Hug Shared Around the World." *CNN*. December 1, 2014. www.cnn.com/2014/11/29/living/ferguson-protest-hug/index.html. Accessed November 24, 2023.

Grippando, James. *Gone Again*. New York: Harper Collins, 2016.

Haasch, Palmer. "Ukrainian Orphan Natalia Grace's Adoptive Parents Accused Her of Being an Adult Who Was Posing as a Child. Where Are Michael and Kristine Barnett Now?" *Business Insider*. January 3, 2024. www.businessinsider.com/natalia-grace-parents-where-are-michael-kristine-barnett-now-2024-1. Accessed January 17, 2024.

Halleen, Toni. *The Surrogate*. New York: Harper Collins, 2021.

Harness, Susan Devan. *Bitterroot: A Salish Memoir of Transracial Adoption*. Lincoln: University of Nebraska Press, 2018.

Hicks, Randall. *Baby Crimes*. San Diego: Wordslinger Press, 2007.

Adopting in America: How to Adopt Within One Year. San Diego: Wordslinger Press, 2018.

Hill, Kashmir. "Whoops. How DNA Site 23andMe Outed Parents Who Gave Their Baby Up for Adoption." *Forbes*. May 16, 2012. www.forbes.com/sites/kashmirhill/2012/05/16/dna-site-23andme-outed-parents-who-gave-their-first-baby-up-for-adoption/?sh=7071e7bb4dd1. Accessed November 19, 2023.

Homans, Margaret, ed. *The Imprint of another Life: Adoption Narratives and Human Possibility*. Ann Arbor, MI: University of Michigan Press, 2013.

"Critical Adoption Studies: Conversation in Progress." *Adoption and Culture*. vol. 6, no.1, 2018, pp. 1–49.

Homes, A. M. *In a Country of Mothers*. New York: Knopf, 1993.

The Mistress' Daughter. New York: Penguin, 2007.

Hsiao, Anna. "The Black Market Behind Adoption in Modern America." *Perspectives in Black Markets*, Vol. 4. Ed. Michael Morrone. Indiana University, 2020. https://iu.pressbooks.pub/perspectives4/chapter/the-black-market-behind-adoption-in-modern-america/. Accessed August 17, 2023.

Huh, Jinny. "On Mothering: Notes from an Asian American Transracial Adoptive Mother." *Adoption and Culture*, vol. 9, no. 2, 2021, pp. 203–218.

Hunter, Christie Craig *In Another Life*. New York: St. Martin's Press, 2019.

Hutcherson, Laraine. *The Boy Detective and the Mystery of Adoption*. N.p., CreateSpace Independent, 2014.

Ito, Susan Kiyo. *I Would Meet You Anywhere*. Columbus, OH: Mad Creek Books, 2023.

Jackson, Rachel. "Provable Connections: On Amanda Jayatissa's 'My Sweet Girl.'" *L.A. Review of Books*. December 6, 2021. https://lareviewofbooks.org/article/provable-connections-on-amanda-jayatissas-my-sweet-girl/. Accessed November 14, 2023.

James, Phyllis Dorothy *Innocent Blood*. New York: Scribner, 1980.

Jeong Trenka, Jane. *The Language of Blood*. Minneapolis, MN: Graywolf Press, 2003.

Fugitive Visions: An Adoptee's Return to Korea. Minneapolis, MN: Graywolf Press, 2009.

Johnson, Kay Ann. *China's Hidden Children*. Chicago: University of Chicago Press, 2016.

Johnson, Lauren. "A Search for Biological Relatives Leads an Adopted Woman to the FBI's Most Wanted List." *CNN*. March 8, 2021. www.cnn.com/ 2021/03/08/us/dna-test-leads-woman-to-her-most-wanted-father-trnd/ index.html. Accessed November 19, 2023.

Kamal, Sheena. *The Lost Ones*. New York, NY: Harper Collins, 2017.

It All Falls Down. New York, NY: William Morrow, 2018.

No Going Back. New York, NY: William Morrow, 2020.

Kane, Ellery. *The Wrong Family*. London: Bookouture, 2023.

Kent, Minka. *The Memory Watcher*. North Haven, CT: Amazon Digital, 2017.

Kernan, Jenna. *The Adoption*. London: Bookouture, 2022.

Kotowski, Jason. "West Trial: Adoptive Parents Found Guilty of 5 of 7 Charges, Including Murder." *KGET*. May 19, 2023. www.kget.com/missing-cal-city-boys/west-trial-trezell-jacqueline-west-found-guilty-5-of-7-charges/. Accessed August 15, 2023.

Lasser, Scott. *The Year That Follows*. New York: Vintage, 2009.

Lee, Jia Sun "The Trauma of Transracial Adoption." *Yes Magazine*. November 13, 2019. www.yesmagazine.org/opinion/2019/11/13/adoption-trauma-trans racial. Accessed November 14, 2023.

Everyone Was Falling. U.S.: Pent Up Press, 2020.

Lee, Julayne. *Not My White Savior: A Memoir in Poems*. Los Angeles, CA: Rare Bird Books, 2018.

Lipitz, Amanda, Producer and Director. *Found*. Amanda Lipitz Productions, Impact Partners, Kindred Spirit, Artemis Rising Foundation, Stick Figure Productions, and Seesaw Productions. 2021.

Marr, Elle. *Strangers We Know*. Seattle: Thomas and Mercer, 2022.

Mohan, Meghan. "Transracial Adoption: I've Been Accused of Kidnapping My White Child." *BBC News*. September 24, 2020. www.bbc.com/news/stor ies-54238642. Accessed November 15, 2023.

Morson, Jenn. "When Families Un-Adopt a Child." *The Atlantic*. November 16, 2018. www.theatlantic.com/family/archive/2018/11/children-who-have-second-adoptions/575902/. Accessed August 16, 2023.

Mosley, Water. *Devil in a Blue Dress*. New York: Norton, 1990.

A Red Death. New York: Washington Square Press, 2010. Originally published 1991.

White Butterfly. New York: Washington Square Press, 2002. Originally published 1992.

Black Betty. New York: Washington Square Press, 2002. Originally published 1994.

Muller, Marcia. *Listen to the Silence.* New York, NY: Warner Books, 2000.

Muller, Wesley. "Anti-Abortion Group Opposes Giving Adopted People Access to Birth Certificates." *Louisiana Illuminator.* March 15, 2022. https://lailluminator.com/2022/03/15/pro-life-group-opposes-giving-adopted-people-access-to-birth-certificates/. Accessed November 19, 2023.

Mullin, Steph & Nicole Mabry. *The Family Tree.* London: Avon. 2021.

National Association of Black Social Workers. "Position Statement on Trans-racial Adoptions." September 1972. https://cdn.ymaws.com/www.nabsw.org/resource/collection/E1582D77-E4CD-4104-996A-D42D08F9CA7D/NABSW_Trans-Racial_Adoption_1972_Position_(b).pdf. Accessed November 18, 2023.

Nelson, Claudia. "'Masked Kidnappers': Representing Adoptive Mothers, 1939-2010." *Adoption & Culture*, vol. 6, no. 1, 2018, pp. 94–115.

Newman, Lily Hay. "23andMe User Data Stolen in Targeted Attack on Ashkenazi Jews." *Wired.* October 6, 2023. www.wired.com/story/23andme-credential-stuffing-data-stolen/. Accessed November 20, 2023.

Ng, Celeste. *Little Fires Everywhere.* New York: Penguin, 2017.

Patterson, James. *Step on a Crack.* New York: Little, Brown, 2007.

Peiser, Jaclyn. "DNA Doesn't Lie. People Lie." *Washington Post.* February 9, 2022. www.washingtonpost.com/magazine/interactive/2022/dna-testing-bryntwick-siblings/. Accessed November 19, 2023.

Phelan, Peggy. "The Dobbs Decision: Abortion, Adoption, and the Supreme Court." *Adoption & Culture*, vol. 10, no. 2, 2022, pp. 171–183.

Rader-Day, Lori. *The Death of Us.* New York, NY: William Morrow, 2023.

Raymond, Barbara Bisantz. *The Baby Thief: The Untold Story of Georgia Tann, the Baby Seller Who Corrupted Adoption.* New York: Carroll and Graf, 2007.

Regalado, Antonio. "More Than 26 Million People Have Taken an At-Home Ancestry Test." *MIT Technology Review.* February 11, 2019. www.technologyreview.com/2019/02/11/103446/more-than-26-million-people-have-taken-an-at-home-ancestry-test/. Accessed November 20, 2023.

Roberts, Dorothy. *Shattered Bonds: The Color of Child Welfare.* New York, NY: Basic Books, 2001.

Torn Apart: How the Child Welfare System Destroys Black Families. New York, NY: Basic Books, 2022.

Rosenhaus, Nancy. "How DNA Tests Are Impacting the World of Adoption." *Adoptions with Love Blog.* June 18, 2019. https://adoptionswithlove.org/uncategorized/dna-tests-impacting-adoption. Accessed November 19, 2023.

Ross, Helen Klein. *What Was Mine.* New York: Gallery Books, 2016.

Scottoline, Lisa. *Look Again.* New York: Macmillan, 2009.

Selk, Avi. "A Teen Reunited with Her Birth Mother – Who Then Killed Her and Burned Her Body On an Isolated Farm in Missouri, Police Say." *The Washington Post.* August 24, 2017. www.washingtonpost.com/news/true-crime/wp/2017/08/23/a-teen-reunited-with-her-birth-mother-who-then-killed-her-and-burned-her-body-police-say/. Accessed November 18, 2023.

Shapiro, Dani. *Inheritance.* New York: Knopf, 2019.

Siegal, Erin. *Finding Fernanda: Two Mothers, One Child, and a Cross-Border Search for Truth.* Boston: Beacon Press, 2011.

Sjöblom, Lisa Wool-Rim. *Palimpsest: Documents from a Korean Adoption.* Canada: Drawn & Quarterly, 2019.

Staub, Wendy Corsi. *Little Girl Lost.* New York: Harper Collins, 2018.

Dead Silence. New York: Harper Collins, 2019.

The Butcher's Daughter. New York: Harper Collins, 2020.

Straley, John. *So Far and Good.* New York: Soho Press, 2021.

Sun, Carolyn. "I'm Asian, My Husband Is White and Our Son Is Black." In the Adoption World, We're a 'Visible Family.' So Why Can't Others See Us?" *Yahoo!Life.* November 5, 2021. www.yahoo.com/lifestyle/im-asian-husband-white-son-black-adoption-visible-family-120042767-130609602.html. Accessed November 15, 2023.

Townsend, Jacinda. "Reclaiming Self-Determination: A Call for Intraracial Adoption." *Duke Journal of Gender Law & Policy*, vol. 2, Spring 1995, pp. 173–190.

Mother Country. Minneapolis, MN: Graywolf Press, 2022.

Trenka, Jane Jeong, Julia Chinyere Oparah, and Sun Yung Shin, eds. *Outsiders Within: Writing on Transracial Adoption.* Cambridge, MA: South End Press, 2006.

Twohey, Megan. "Americans Use the Internet to Abandon Children Adopted from Overseas." *Reuters Investigates.* September 9, 2013. www.reuters.com/investigates/adoption/#article/part1. Accessed August 16, 2023.

Umrigar, Thrity. *Everybody's Son.* New York: Harper Collins, 2017.

VanSickle, Abbie. "Supreme Court Upholds Native American Adoption Law." *New York Times.* June 15, 2023. www.nytimes.com/2023/06/15/us/

supreme-court-native-american-children-tribes.html. Accessed November 17, 2023.

Vargas, Ramon Antonio. "Six-Year-Old Orphan or 'Con-Artist' Adult? Revisiting the Strange Story of Natalia Grace." *The Guardian.* June 4, 2023. www .theguardian.com/us-news/2023/jun/04/natalia-grace-docuseries-hbo-discov ery-ukrainian-orphan-con-artist. Accessed August 15, 2023.

Wheat, Carolyn. *Fresh Kills.* New York: Open Road, 1995.

Wilde, Jennifer Hanlon. *Finding the Vein.* Portland, OR: Ooligan Press, 2021.

Wills, Jenny Heijun. "Formulating Kinship: Asian Adoption Narratives and Crime Literature." *Adoption & Culture*, vol. 5, 2017, pp. 64–88.

　Older Sister, Not Necessarily Related. Canada: McClelland & Stewart, 2019.

Wingate, Lisa. *Before We Were Yours.* New York: Ballantine, 2017.

Cambridge Elements ≡

Crime Narratives

Margot Douaihy

Emerson College

Margot Douaihy, PhD, is an assistant professor at Emerson College in Boston. She is the author of *Scorched Grace* (Gillian Flynn Books/Zando, 2023), which was named one of the best crime novels of 2023 by *The New York Times*, *The Guardian*, and *CrimeReads*. Her recent scholarship includes "Beat the Clock: Queer Temporality and Disrupting Chrononormativity in Crime Fiction," a NeMLA 2024 paper.

Catherine Nickerson

Emory College of Arts and Sciences

Catherine Ross Nickerson is the author of *The Web of Iniquity: Early Detective Fiction by American Women* (Duke University Press, 1999), which was nominated for an Edgar Award by the Mystery Writers of America. She is the editor of *The Cambridge Companion to American Crime Fiction* (2010), as well as two volumes of reprinted novels by Anna Katharine Green and Metta Fuller Victor (Duke University Press).

Henry Sutton

University of East Anglia

Henry Sutton, SFHEA, is Professor of Creative Writing and Crime Fiction at the University of East Anglia. He is the author of fifteen novels, including two crime fiction series. His is also the author of the *Crafting Crime Fiction* (Manchester University Press, 2023) and the co-editor of *Domestic Noir: The New Face of 21st Century Crime Fiction* (Palgrave Macmillan, 2018).

Advisory Board

About the Series

Publishing groundbreaking research from scholars and practitioners of crime writing in its many dynamic and evolving forms, this series examines and re-examines crime narratives as a global genre which began on the premise of entertainment, but quickly evolved to probe pressing political and sociological concerns, along with the human condition.

Cambridge Elements ☰

Crime Narratives

Elements in the Series

Forensic Crime Fiction
Aliki Varvogli

Female Anger in Crime Fiction
Caroline Reitz

Crime Fiction and Ecology: From the Local to the Global
Nathan Ashman

Bloodlines: Adoption, Crime, and the Search for Belonging
Jinny Huh

A full series listing is available at: www.cambridge.org/ECNA